WHO SAYS YOU CAN'T SELL ICE TO ESKIMOS?

A Door-to-Door Salesman Reveals the Timeless Secrets of Selling Anybody, Anything

by

James W. Murphy

Foreword: James D. Murphy
Edited by L. Douglas Keeney
Copyedited by Carl Arnold, www.edit1to1.com
Cover Design: Lone Red Design, www.lonered.com
Photos courtesy: The Author
For bulk copies contact:
www.douglaskeeney.com
ISBN-13: 978-1490365251
ISBN-10: 1490365257
Library of Congress Control Number: 2013910375
CreateSpace Independent Publishing Platform
North Charleson, SC

James W. Murphy

Brief Biography

Born on August 5, 1938, in Lexington Kentucky, Jim Murphy has spent a lifetime pursuing the skills of the sale. He started his career as an IBM salesman in the North Florida territory selling the IBM Selectric typewriter, which débuted in the early 1960s. Jim's outstanding performance as an IBM salesman caught the eye of the Florida branch manager for World Book Encyclopedia, owned by the Field Enterprises Corporation.

This is where Jim spent the bulk of his selling career as a door-to-door salesman, eventually breaking records and establishing himself as a successful branch manager. He earned the company's highest awards in all categories — individual selling, service, recruiting and branch management. Some of his achievements at World Book included: the Superior Service Key Award, the Tree of Life Award (the company's highest award for superiority in recruiting), the division manager's Flying Circus recipient (the company's highest overall sales honor) and an appointment to World Book's President's Advisory Council.

Jim hired and trained over a thousand salespeople, a significant accomplishment for any company. He then took over branch operations in Kentucky, where his team consistently drove more than $5 million in sales revenue each year until he retired at the early age of 51. He then invested in the Toshiba copier and facsimile dealership in this area of the country and quickly grew that business into four offices and over eight million dollars in annual sales. Jim sold that company in the late 1990s and retired to his horse farm in Shelbyville, Kentucky.

Introduction

by James D. Murphy

My father was from the last great generation of salesmen. He grew up in the scotch and cigarettes era, doing the least glamorous job in America: door-to-door sales for IBM, World Book Encyclopedia, and later on, Toshiba. It wasn't flashy work, but he loved it, and he made a great life for my mom and my sisters in Shelbyville, Kentucky. We eventually settled on a horse farm that was paid for one fifty-dollar commission at a time, one five hundred-dollar sale at a time, five million dollars in sales a year. That's a lot of money, but that's a lot of selling too.

Dad loved it. He knocked on tens of thousands of doors and pitched in the living rooms of American families in Florida, Massachusetts, Ohio, Indiana, and Kentucky. Selling was something he had a gift for but, like the rest of us, he had to learn some skills too. His indoctrination came in 1963 at IBM. At that time, it was probably the best sales force in the world. From getting past the secretaries to closing with the boss, they taught him how to sell typewriters and office equipment — long before you bought those things in a grocery cart at Target or Best Buy.

Dad's boss at IBM had a client who was a dynamic guy with a yacht in Florida who owned the World Book franchise for the entire state. This person was good for an IBM machine or two a year, but Dad was hungry for more and he saw what was going on down there with encyclopedias. It didn't happen overnight, but in 1969, Dad called him and said he wanted to get on board with World Book. He stuck with it for the next twenty-two years.

At that time, World Book was a national organization subdivided into seventy-three different branches, including the one Dad eventually owned in Kentucky. World Book had thousands of people going door-to-door every day. Their collective experience refined the sales process into an exact science. It was paint-by-numbers, sell-by-numbers. Every action had an equal and opposite reaction that got you closer to *yes*. What if the dad answers the door? What if mom answers? If the kids are in the room for the sales pitch, how do you keep them interested?

World Book had wormholes and alleyways for every possible direction a conversation might take. It was a script that the company had perfected over decades, and my dad — having not only sold himself, but having trained hundreds of other salesmen — knew it cold. He knew the objections, he knew the value propositions, and he could tell by the way you turned a book's pages whether you were ready for the close or not.

He developed an eye for detail that kept him two steps ahead of every sale. He knew the tricks that you can learn only on the pavement, going door-to-door for a lifetime. He made a sport out of it. It was always fun. It was always a mental game. I remember him at dinner, often talking about how to navigate this puzzle, this psychological puzzle that was called "the American family." Twice he won World Book's highest award — the Flying Circus — the MVP award for the entire company. And when he was tired of selling encyclopedias, he started his own company selling copiers, and then sold it for seven million dollars.

World Book became part of our family. I grew up thinking "prospect, canvas, cold call, close." You closed the deal, you got paid. A true rip 'em and stick 'em mentality. As a young kid, he gave me *How to Win Friends and Influence People* — one of the original editions. It was an old, dusty hardback. He was always a big reader of books on selling.

Dad carried his A Volume everywhere. When you signed on as a World Book salesman, they gave you this nice briefcase, and in it was the A Volume. The thickest volume in the set of 22, it was the demo volume. So it had more science, more detail in it than the others. We always had a full set of World Books in the house. He believed in the product so much that he referred any dinner conversation right back to it. "Go look it up, son," was his answer to most questions, and then I'd have to scour the house for whatever spine-creased volume we needed — inevitably under someone's bed or the kitchen counter — before the conversation could move on.

His instruction didn't stop there. Each of his three kids — including me — was raised on the art of selling. It was like learning to catch a ball. From an early age, we knew Dad's five-step process: you prospect, you canvas your territory, you cold call, you demo, and you close. No appointments, no call-backs, and no gimmicks. When we became sales-men ourselves, we already understood that orders came only when we'd executed each of these five steps.

Dad had a passion for teaching — teaching the art of pitching and closing — and that's what this book is mainly about. He trained and hired every single person who ever worked for him. His passion was for delivering sales — training salespeople and showing them the art of selling and closing. See, Dad knew that if you could get the script right, if you could learn the territory, and if you could handle the inevitable rejection, then it was only matter of time before you got to *yes*. That was the promise he made to every salesman he ever hired — a promise he backed up with his own cash. Do it right and do it a lot, and the money will come. If not, Dad would write you a check for the commission that the numbers said you should have made. That's how deeply he believed in a disciplined sales process.

It's 2013 now, and Solution Selling and driving toward "trusted advisor" status are so important. But in truth, we've lost more than a generation of salesmen. The accumulated knowledge of Dad's door-to-door army of thousands is mostly gone, but its importance remains. While most modern sales forces hide behind technology to avoid the tough side of selling — the canvassing, the cold calls, and the close — they're doing it at their own expense. They're leaving money on the table because they've forgotten the fundamentals of relationship building and closing. It's been a while since Dad knocked on someone's door but there's still no substitute for human contact: person-to-person, one order at a time, $500 a sale, $5 million a year.

Selling was a game for Dad and sales was about winning the psychological battle beneath it. We talked about it every night at dinner — as father and son and as CEO and branch manager. And when we were done laughing at all the ways we'd embarrassed ourselves to get that order, Dad would say, "Sales are nothing." What he meant was, if you know your script, you know their objections, and you've done your homework, you can sell ice to Eskimos.

Jim Murphy is the son of the author, and the founder and CEO of Afterburner, Inc., a worldwide, multimillion-dollar consultancy firm. He graduated from the University of Kentucky and worked for his father selling copiers before joining the Georgia Air National Guard, where he became a pilot of the prestigious F-15 Eagle air superiority fighter. He eventually became an instructor pilot in the Air Force before starting his own company. Jim is the author of two business bestsellers, Business is Combat *and* Flawless Execution.

Chapter 1

Jim Murphy

Parachute me in. I'm serious. You can give me a World Book sales book and an order pad, and parachute me anywhere in the English-speaking world, and I'll guarantee, in eight hours, I'll have a minimum of one order — and probably three. Guaranteed. We had people selling in Hawaii. We had people selling in England. They were in Germany. Italy was a big place. Australia. Selling is big — worldwide and universal. If they speak English, you parachute me in there with a World Book sales book and an order pad, I'll guarantee you, before the day's over, I'll have a minimum of one order. If it's a good day, I'll have three.

My name is James Murphy, Jim to my friends, Murph to most. I was born into a family of entrepreneurs, salesmen really. My mother was from downtown New York City. Her dad owned the largest theater company in New York — this was before Hollywood. It was vaudeville. My grandfather was an agent in vaudeville. My mother had a chauffeur, an upstairs chambermaid, downstairs chambermaid — all of that.

Somehow my dad, a country boy from Kentucky, a really shy boy, wooed her away. They got married. He brought her down to Lexington, Kentucky and inherited his father's business, which at the time was the

1

largest trucking company in the country. Nineteen forty-five, had 300 trucks, 150 semis on the road. There were a thousand people on the payroll.

I went to Lexington Catholic High School. Our science laboratory — I don't even think we had a microscope. I remember we had Bunsen burners. Had no gym. We used to go up to another school and practice, and had our games over at the junior high school. I mean, my school was nothing. But, I'm telling you, I think something like 75 percent of the people I graduated with — there were only 22 in my class — ended up going to college, and I think 50 percent of them graduated. So their academics were good. I mean, you know, you had to learn. If you didn't, they'd call your parents, and your parents, they'd kick you out. The nuns used to crack my hands with a ruler. It was a different learning experience than what the kids go through today. I mean, you *had* to learn.

I had a paper route through high school, because my dad was not the kind of guy that would flip me any money to go buy a car. He said, "Hey, Son, if you're going to buy a car, get out, get your butt on that bike, and get a paper route." So, I had a rural route and drove it on a motorcycle. I worked all the horse farms.

Then I worked in a gas station. And then, when I graduated from high school, I quickly tasted some success in the construction industry. I was very entrepreneurial, and so I bought a backhoe, started my own construction company. Two years out of high school, I've got a brand-new Cadillac. First backhoe for hire in the city of Lexington. Had it for two and a half, almost three years.

If I'd had it my way, I'd never have finished college and just run my own business forever. I dropped out of college in my freshman year and Eisenhower was the president, threw open the draft, because there was something called the Suez Crisis. When Egypt and Israel went to war, we thought we were going in. He activated the draft, so I had to go back to college. So I went back to college, met my lovely wife Ann, got out of college, got married.

I absolutely never gave selling a thought. I was a senior in college, and a good friend of mine — a heck of a basketball player on a Transylvania College scholarship — got a job with IBM, and he said, "Murph, when you graduate, you really ought to come to IBM. You really ought to."

I said, "What? Selling? I don't want to be selling. Hell, I'm going to be a coach."

"No, you ought to think about it," he said. I think he told me he made $22,000 his first year, so I said, "Whoa! Tell me a little bit more." So I went up and interviewed with a guy named Kelly, but they didn't hire me. They hired a guy the day before I got there. Kelly was interviewing about ten people, and he got sold on this one person. They wrote me a beautiful letter. "Gee, we just don't think you're suitable to do our type of work, and you'd be more suitable to do something else."

Well, I went back up there. I was a pretty feisty kid. I said, "Look, you can't tell me a company the size of IBM doesn't have any more openings than this one opening you're talking about." I said, "I want to see your boss." That shocked the hell out of him. So he picked up the phone and called a man by the name of Tom in Atlanta, on Peachtree Avenue. Tom said, "I want you to come down to see me. We're going to fly you down." So I went down, bought me a new blue serge suit and got me a white shirt. That was the first time I'd been on a plane, when I flew to Atlanta.

IBM took me to lunch, did a half-hour interview, shook my hand, told me I was a nice fellow and that was that. So, I'm leaving, heading

3

back to the airport. And I tell that cab driver, "Pull this cab over to that telephone booth. IBM spent a hundred dollars to fly me down here. I spent fifty dollars for this suit, had a free lunch, an hour interview, and I still don't know if I have a job or not." Well, I had nothing to lose. I *didn't* have a job. What am I going to lose? So I called him back. I said, "Look, I interviewed with you. Do I have the job or not?"

He said, "Boy, you called me back. You do. But if you hadn't called me back, you wouldn't. You go see Tom Kelly, and tell him I said for you to see him Monday morning."

So I went back to see Kelly, and he said, "Well, he's already called me. You've got a job with IBM in Florida. You want to go to Florida?"

Me? Florida? Hell, yes. So that's how that came about. I became a door-to-door IBM salesman in 1963, a job I had for six years. But most everyone thought it was a bad idea. Door-to-door salesmen were lower than used-car salesmen or attorneys. At the end of World War II all these veterans came back from the war and they couldn't find a job. So, I mean, they became hard-core salespeople. They were good. But as they graduated out, as they moved up — this is now in the 1950s and later — the scum of the earth came in behind them. And suddenly there were all kinds of problems with door-to-door. They all turned to Fuller Brush and whatever — pots and pans and selling door-to-door. Now, these were real scum of the Earth. I mean, the tricks — the foot in the door, pushy, that kind of stuff. When I came along, which was twenty years later, that stuff had filtered out. Now they were smarter. They had taken all of those things that worked and put it together.

Next I worked for Marshall Field. That's the World Book Company. And it was straight, up and down the line. No trade-ins, no deals, no discounts, no gimmicks, and we hired mostly teachers and preachers and housewives. So it was straight as an arrow. The stigma was still there, but it was more polished. People still associated door-to-door salesman with tricks and really the scum of the Earth. That's why I say my wife was ready to divorce me. My dad would just sit there and shake his head, "Wasted four years of college."

Anyway, back at IBM, I had to train to be a salesman. I was going to be selling typewriters, dictating machines, and other office products. I was with the Office Products division; it wasn't with the computers. Typewriters and dictating machines. They came out with the forerunner of the storage typewriter. They had a lot of printing equipment, called composers, and typesetting equipment. When I went with them, they'd just announced the Selectric typewriter. That's when I learned the word *quota*.

When I first started, I had to sell 15 typewriters and two dictating machines a month. A typewriter, back then, was around five hundred bucks. Dictating machine was about the same. Six years later, I think it was twenty-five a month plus five or six dictating machines, a composer, and one MTST, which was the forerunner of the storage typewriters, about the size of a desk. Took a girl three days to learn how to operate its magnetic tape. So we had to sell one of those a month. So the quotas were getting tighter and tougher, tighter and tougher.

But I made quota every year. You didn't have to make quota every month, but year to date. If you wanted to hang around, you couldn't miss them, I'll tell you that. But I made it every year.

IBM was a good place to start. I liked what I was doing but over the years it became clear that it wasn't the best fit. IBM didn't take care of its people well enough and the money wasn't as good as it could have been. There was a better job somewhere. See, my boss used to tell me, when he'd get about half drunk, he'd say, "Look, five of you salesmen could get together and get me fired. Three customer complaints could get me fired." He said, "I'm just walking a tightrope. You know, I've got to be nice to salesmen, got to be nice to customers."

So I thought, jeez, I don't know if I want that job or not. See, back when he hired me, I said, "I want your job." And after I was around for three or four years, I said, "I don't think I want his job." I'm working, you know, 38 hours a week, making $24,000. He's working 50 and making $29,000. After taxes, what are we talking about? Five thousand dollars difference? And I've got peace of mind, you know. I don't think I wanted his job.

Well, his best friend was making $129,000. And he had the World Book Branch franchise for the state of Florida. And every time we'd miss quota at the end of the month, my boss would go over and have a couple of drinks, and he said, "What in the hell am I doing?" He said, "If I had a brain in my head, I'd be selling World Book."

Well, I'm a young kid, listening to this stuff, you know. This World Book man and my boss are best friends. They were very, very good friends, so I'd go to lunch with this guy — in fact, he was a customer of mine. I'll tell you, he always had a Buick parked in front of the curb. And he'd get a brand new one every two years. And, on many occasions, he'd kid me and say, "You want to make some good money, come to work with us . . ." da-da-da, he went on. So just on a whim, I called this guy. I went down to Miami, Florida, and he had a cherry red Cadillac sitting in front of his office. And I came in, I said, "Dick, I thought you had company here."

He said, "Why?"

I said, "I see that Cadillac and —"

He said, "Oh, that's mine."

I said, "When did you switch to Cadillac?"

He said, "Hell, the company gave it to me."

I said, "Company gave it to you? What for?"

He said, "Meeting quota."

We used to meet quota at IBM and get a pat on the back or a trophy. I never heard of such a thing. Going back to '67, '68, '69. People just didn't give Cadillacs away.

This World Book salesman was a customer, and occasionally I'd go with my boss and meet him for lunch. And he'd say, "Here, let me pick up the — you can't afford it. If you were selling World Book, you could afford this check, but you . . ."

He used to say, "Oh, if you want to make some big money, you ought to come and work for us" in front of my boss.

Well, I thought that was just a parody — a joke. And it was just in the back of my mind. And I thought, jeez criminy! This guy don't do crap, making $129,000 a year. My boss works 50 hours a week and he's making less than 30K.

It took me three years, I think, to get up to $24,000 with IBM. Average teacher was making $5,000 then. Branch manager was making $129,000 — at World Book. My boss at IBM, been with them 15 years, making $29,000. That was the top 10 percent of the income ladder. And this guy was making over a hundred — that's when postage stamps were a nickel and you could hire a secretary for 35 bucks a week. I mean, that was real money, back then.

Well, I didn't go to World Book right away. I left IBM, but I didn't quit; I left on a temporary leave. I was going to take over my dad's business in Lexington. He had bought into a business college and I was going to help. I was 27, 28 years old and I just hated it. So it was just on a whim — I just picked up the phone and called this guy in Florida. And I said, "Dick, Jim Murphy. I'm thinking about coming back to Florida. I'm missing the sunshine, and I don't want to go back to IBM." I said, "My young son is four years old. I've got about two years where I can knock around and take a chance on something." If it didn't work, since I never quit IBM, I could always go back. In fact, they came to Lexington and tried to hire me back, and I didn't want to go back. So it was just a whim. I had two years before my son was in the first grade — and that's when I went with World Book.

It wasn't easy money. I took a pay cut to get started at World Book but the returns were there once I learned the business. In the last year at IBM, I made probably 22, 23 thousand dollars. In the first year at World Book, I made $16,000. In my second year, I made $30,000. And my third year, $50,000. Within three years, I had doubled my salary. It was a great job. Pure selling. No wheeling and dealing. World Book, no deals. No trade-ins, no discounts, no gimmicks, nothing — cash. Cash. Money up front.

I started in Tampa and then went to Jacksonville. Started in Tampa as a district manager and then went to Jacksonville as a division manager in training. I went to training for four years to be a division manager. As a district manager in Florida, I had two part-time area managers, and probably 40 people in my group. We worked strictly with part-time people. Free agents only. Now, once you became full-time under the Marshall Field Company, which was World Book's parent company, then you got into their profit-sharing. I mean, plus their insurance — it was fantastic. I was promoted to Jacksonville in two years, as division manager, which meant I took over six full-time managers and probably a hundred people

8

up there in northern Florida. I was there two years, and then they made me a national trainer and a turn-around specialist.

So they needed me in Boston for two years   well, northern New England, really. I was working out of Boston, but I had a little bit of New York — what else is up there? — Rhode Island, New Hampshire. There were 73 state offices — we called them branches. And Boston was 73rd in sales. I mean, it was the worst. I was there two years and moved it up to 56th or 57th. And, then, from there, they sent me to another under-performer — Ohio. I had all across Lake Erie there, from Cleveland — I lived over around Toledo, a little town called Maumee, just a little bitty community; and I was there two years. We took that one from about 71st and moved it up to about 31st. There was a little problem, though. I wanted to go back to Florida, where I'd cut my teeth and all my kids were born and raised. I hated the cold, the snow, the blizzard of '78. And this son of a gun gave the territory — the Florida territory — to someone else. So I went over his head, to the president of the company. I heard Kentucky was opening up, and gave him chapter and verse on not getting Florida and all the reasons why I should get Kentucky. The offices I managed and turned around were proof that I should get my own branch, one of my choosing. I built an organization with hundreds of reps earning commission for themselves and for me. Everybody was door-to-door. I knocked on thousands of doors, interviewed thousands of reps. I made a lot of sales door-to-door.

Well, I got it. I was a branch manager in Kentucky for eight years. I ran about 350 or 400 full-time sales reps. My first two or three years, I was really selling, because I needed the money to raise kids. I was selling $100, $150,000 of World Books a year. And the best year, I think, was $180,000. That was in '84, '85, '86 — somewhere around there.

Anyway, bit by bit we got bigger. On a yearly basis, we did 5,000,000 bucks. A sale was usually 500 bucks, on average. So we were doing $5,000,000 a year on $500 sales. Before I got there, this branch was doing probably a million and a half. Million and a half.

People started to notice the volume my offices were doing. It was a big deal. Company gave me a trophy. It had an angel on it with two little kids, and it's got the numbers on it, my numbers. Top-performing manager in the system.

So I started getting calls, opportunities. Other jobs were calling.

I said, "Come on, now." I liked World Book. I believed in the product. I liked selling. Even as a manager, I still went door-to-door. I was door-to-door "forever" during my 22 years at World Book. But, as a branch manager, I wasn't supposed to, but I did it on occasion, you know, just to pick up some extra money. Shoot, I'd set up a fair booth or something, you know, a real booth at a real state fair, with a table, and put some books on it and some signage and I'd take pictures of people that came by, post them — lets them come back and see their pictures. I'd put out a big box, with a slot, wrap the box in Christmas paper — do a drawing for a free World Book. I'd talk to everyone, get a feel for them, then all of a sudden I had 50 names, 50 leads. I'd call them up, make an appointment, and go sell them. Just like picking cherries.

People forget to do fair booths. You have to think of every angle. But the rest of the time, if you don't have any names, you've got to go out and knock on a door. So, I was out selling every day.

But a manager wasn't supposed to be selling that hard. I made about a thousand sales on my own before I had to hang it up. They finally convinced me, my job is not to sell books. All salespeople reach that stage.

It's how you make the big jump. "Your job is to hire and train and show other people how to sell.

But it was the selling that I loved. I believed in the product and I loved the work. Years later, it's still the selling that I remember most. You know, it's funny, the most successful people all ended up being branch managers and when we got together and did a bunch of drinking, all we'd talk about is the old days and walking down the street — the fun we used to have and the execution, the mind games we had to play to win the order. We didn't talk about being a branch manager.

It's not the end point, it's the trip there. That's what people talk about. It's just like it was being a wing commander for my son, he's an Air Force pilot. When they get together, I mean, they don't talk about, you know, the budgets and the new technologies that are coming. They talk about flying, what it was like being deployed, about pilot training. You know, the real world, walking the streets knocking on doors, where it's up to you to get the job done.

It's the door-to-door salesman's skill and discipline that eventually let me run my own company. I finally sold copiers door-to-door for Triple M — Murphy Murphy Murphy, a company my brother and I bought. We had the Toshiba copier franchise. Built it like crazy and sold it for seven million. It was estimated at nine million. We ended up selling for seven.

The lessons of door-to-door sales are timeless. There're so many singles you had to hit to be successful in this industry. I mean, you had to be Ty Cobb, you had to hit a million singles. Pete Rose, instead of being a home-run hitter all the time, having a couple of big number years, you have to do it year in and year out. People are still selling today, but door-to-door's gone. I sit in a plane and hear the talk around me. Farm equipment, lighting, cars — it's still people-to-people and we learned how to do it in the most hostile environment there is. Knocking on a door. Uninvited. But we learned what works and people are people. Parachute me in with an order pad and I'll get one, at least one.

And it all started because I said to myself, "I'm going to give it a shot. I have nothing to lose. I'm going to call and ask for that job."

It all started because I did the first thing you got to do in selling: I sold myself.

Chapter 2

Territories, Relationships, and Bluebirds — How to Avoid Salesman Solitary

As a starting salesman, they'd put you out in the boondocks. And you earned your money there and then. When I started at IBM, I had the North Florida territory, places like Lake City or Palatka, Florida. More snakes and alligators than people. Made no sense. I was in the smallest territories, the smallest cities in state. One time I was in an office and there was a mounted Eastern Diamondback rattlesnake. The owner didn't tell me so I sit down with him — he was in insurance — and I turned around and see this mouth of this snake in the strike position. Scared me to death.

Anyway, thirty years later, when I was managing Triple M, the copier business, we would look at a territory and see what the potential was. In other words, if there's 50 copy machines there, there's 10 Xerox, 10 Sharps, 10 Canon — so there ought to be room for 5 Toshibas. But with IBM, I just had the smallest, the hardest towns to cut my teeth on. You really had to work it.

Now, we look at a territory and say, "Well, this is the potential of it." And that would equal so much revenue for the company. Therefore, if you're getting ten percent as your commission, that would be your potential income as a salesman. Might be a little better, might be a little worse, but that's what we're shooting for. And we'd sit down and try to sell our reps on this particular territory and show them what, probably, would be minimum — probably the maximum. "This is what we're shooting for. Is this agreeable with you?"

I'm sure I kidded some people along the way — took a crappy territory and told the newbie's how great it was. But, overall, I knew, if we were going to keep them, you've got to be up-front with them. If you're just turning and burning and getting your salespeople out the back door quick as you can get them in the front door, then it didn't matter. But, see, with Triple M, we were looking for full-time career people. We were pretty straight up with them.

Working a territory is a science — it takes precision

I always had my people split up a territory into four parts — either four ZIP codes, four city blocks, or four counties, or whatever the territory was. So, you take your territory and split it in four equal parts — Monday, Tuesday, Wednesday, Thursday, leaving Friday open, as a runaround day, delivering literature, delivering demos, following up on this or that, training someone. It's just your runaround day. What that day does, is it saves you from running your commission out your exhaust pipe. 'Cause that's what happens with most salespeople.

So when you start on Monday, working in that territory, you didn't leave it for hell. Even if someone said, "My sister-in-law, in Territory 2, wants to buy," we'd say, "Well, she's not planning on moving in the next three days is she? I work that territory on Thursday. I'll be down there Thursday." Most people run out of Territory 1 and run over to Territory 3. When you're in Territory 1, you don't leave it until you have three reasons to come back next week. You work all day long to have three appointments, three places you're going to drop off literature, three demos, three something. You've got to have a reason, a planned purpose, a *callback*.

Then you work Territory 2. And you don't leave it till you have three reasons to come back next Tuesday — callbacks. And so on for Wednesday and Thursday. Callbacks are in place. So you have a reason to go, a place to start next week. And then Friday was my runaround day. Go back into the territory, pick up orders, do other administrative stuff.

If you don't manage a territory efficiently, you're going to get lost in the game of chasing lousy leads or doing nothing at all. There's no substitute for grunt work, volume, and discipline. Most salesmen are just looking for a friendly door. Looking for the best door. In other words, every green door is the best one.

If you have a quota of 15 machines a month, you've got to get an order every two days. And you didn't sell too many multiples back then, unless you had a big bank or something. We'd sell one today and come back in a month and sell the second one in there, come back a month later and sell a third one. But very rarely could you come in and get an order for three.

See, the interstates wasn't even in. When I went down to Lake City, Florida, I used to go down on old Route 25, through Mikesville. I mean, interstates just weren't there. About five miles out of town, there was nothing but timber, a lot of big, big timber companies that had thousands — literally, thousands of acres of pine trees. Lot of dirt roads — sand roads down there, a lot of them. Occasionally, you'd see a big tower for the forest ranger but nothing but pine trees, pine trees, pine trees. You'd go for, like, 40 miles between towns.

You'd stay in a Howard Johnson, Holiday Inn, probably 22 bucks a night or something. They didn't have any big hotels. You go to a downtown hotel — had to carry your own luggage in. But Howard Johnson's was the big one, and Holiday Inn was just coming on strong, so they were becoming available down South. So that was kind of the run-of-the-mill type place we'd stay in.

Vertical marketing

In small towns, like Lake City, Florida, the key to success was usually though the government offices, where there's guaranteed to be a purchasing budget and a need for books and office equipment. Mostly county, city, state government, because IBM had a good name with them. And I tried to make buddies with the county clerk, who generally swung a lot of weight in a courthouse; and then, independent lawyers, attorneys, newspapers, chambers of commerce — whoever uses banks — those people were down the street, they'd fall into place after that county clerk. But my first stop, generally, was to try and tie in with county government or state government, because we generally had a government-only catalog. We had a base and, you know, we were pretty much accepted there.

Being accepted was not a given. In fact, in Lake City it was hard earned. I remember, in Lake City, I covered that place like a glove. One of the two people I really knew down there was the sheriff, who came to me my first day or two in the territory, and said, "Well, I understand you don't have a license to sell your equipment here in Lake City."

And I said, "Well, who told you that?" And there's the Underwood typewriter dealer, sitting there, looking out the window. And I said, "I know who told you."

And he said, "Well, are you a member of our chamber?"

And I said, "No."

He said, "Well, you don't need a license if you're a member of our chamber."

And I said, "Well, IBM's a national member of the Chamber of Commerce. We're in every city in the United States. I don't need to join this local one, do I?"

And he said, "Well, if you don't, the Better Business Bureau's going to put you on the crap list. And if you're on that, you can't sell here. And it's up to me to make sure you're not selling here." Little one-horse town. The Chamber of Commerce and the Better Business Bureau were in bed together. And that's true in almost every town. Check it out — they're in the same office, one upstairs, one downstairs. They're in bed together.

So, anyway, I made a buddy out of the guy. Everybody knew him. Just a gregarious, outgoing guy. And if he patted you on the back, you're all right, you're all right in that town.

The second guy was president of the bank — he was an attorney. Young guy. Every day I went into Lake City, I'd stop by there and bring his secretary a cup of coffee or stop by to talk to him, or something. And he bought just two or three pieces of equipment. He wasn't a big, big buyer. But he helped me get in the courthouse and, I mean, he was just so well known. It was the biggest bank in town.

So, do you see a pattern here? You start with the key influencers, the people who lead you to more people and things start to roll.

Now, you'll also notice I didn't make appointments. Never made one. Never made an appointment in all the time I was at IBM. *Never* made an appointment. It was pull up to the courthouse and canvass,

17

gather information, find the end user, and take them by surprise. Look at the sign, see their names, go up there. Talk to a janitor, talk to a maid, talk to a meter maid. "What's the county clerk's name? What's he do?"

"Oh, he kind of kowtows to the judge."

"Oh, what's the judge's name?"

"Well, they're kind of in bed together with the sheriff."

"Well, what's his name? Who swings weight around here — the sheriff? Well, let me go talk to him. What's his secretary's name?"

Just go in and start gathering information, then try and get in and talk to the sheriff or the judge. I always worked on the theory I'm not going to wait over 30 minutes to see anybody, because it's just a waste of time.

Grow the network from there. Make friends with anyone who talks. Vertical marketing. I think people ought to learn how to do that — in their own territory, not have the company do it for them. Getting known is the most important thing to do if you're working a territory over a long period of time. Get to know the mailman, the UPS man and the FedEx man and the janitor and the, you know, the local sheriff.

Now, I learned that in Boston, which was the worst territory World Book had. That's the reason they sent me up there. And this old boy said to me, "Murph, there ain't no way in hell you're going to go into downtown Boston and take care of Rhode Island, New Hampshire, and the whole state of Massachusetts," he says. "It's just too encompassing. You break that thing down into four days. And when you get into inner Boston, go just for the Irish Catholics or just for the Jewish community or just for the Italian community, and you stay there until you develop influence through the churches and schools and principals, and hire local people. And don't leave that territory. And then, when you

18

go to New Hampshire, you know, just go to the farming community, or whatever it may be." And that's what I did for two years. And we took that thing from 73rd up to, like, 51st or something. Not bad for a southern boy. I mean, a real southern boy, bad southern accents and all, in inner city Boston. Never seen snow before, my kids being called on in class just to hear them talk and count, make fun of them. But I turned that around from the seventies up 20 places, door-to-door in their homes, accent and all.

There is always a broader network — a civic group, a church, something — that you can access for referrals, leads, and the next sale. In World Book, it was the educational community — churches, people of influence, colleges, etc. When I was with IBM, going out in little towns in North Florida like Lake City, Rayford, Palatka, it was very, very important to become known as the IBM salesman in that community. You did that by speaking and going and having lunch every day, at the same counter, meeting the postman, meeting the janitor, the local policeman, the mayor of — the little sheriffs, and all this stuff. Same counter every day until they say "Hello, Mr. Murphy" when you sit down and order coffee. Name-dropping — very, very important working in the rural community.

At World Book, hiring salespeople was key to my duties. Recruiting, recruiting, recruiting. I loved to drop into churches to meet the pastor. "Hi, Pastor. I'm working around your neighborhood. And I'm sure there's some lady in your choir, or maybe a widow that's living on restricted means, and we've got an opportunity to work part time, and its education too. And she can make some extra money. And I'd like to ask if you would introduce her to me. Could you introduce me to her?" Oh, yeah, yeah. No problem. Same thing with schools.

So, how does this pay off?

On a cold call in that neighborhood, I see the King James Bible on the table, and think I have a bible-thumper here. Well, you know, close to a Baptist church, stands to reason I might get lucky. "Well, do you know Reverend Holtram? I was just up there, visiting him. He doesn't have World Book for his kid, but he wants to get one." Or take it this way. "Call Reverend Holtram. He knows about it." It kind of cements the trust issue — "Well, you're okay, if you're a friend of Reverend Holtram." No big deal. Just kind of name-dropping. It doesn't hurt. Isn't going to get you an order, but it's a start.

Being known is about being outgoing

Say hello. Make friends. Talk. Be respectful whenever you can. Always be selling. I still do it. A good friend of mine — he sells sports equipment — and we went to lunch together. I went to pay the check, and there was two old boys sitting there, and I got to joking with them. I didn't know them from a hole in the wall. Well, my friend is impatient, he's hurrying me on. "Come on, Murph! Damn it! You talk to everybody." And I'm just kidding the guy. He had a big dessert. I don't even remember what it was. I said, "My God! You going to eat all that?"

And he said, "Yeah."

And I said, "Well, could I have a bite?" And he started laughing. We just started jacking. Do it all the time. Do it all the time. Point is, my buddy, who's still selling, he should be doing that too. I think it's very important. Meet people. Start conversations.

When I was working inside of Jacksonville, Florida, there were a couple of guys that I knew and I swapped leads with them. One guy was selling calculators, which used to be a full-time job. He made good money doing that. Another guy was selling printing equipment. But any of those guys selling calculators, we just met for lunch or for coffee and shoot the bull and talk about a ballgame or something and then something comes out like, "What have you got that's hot?"

"Well, I'm working on something. Bank told me they're going to open up a branch down here."

So it wasn't a weekly, daily, monthly thing but we did it on purpose and we all knew we were doing it to trade leads. Most salespeople forget that stuff and it's important.

You need at least three good leads to move on to the next quadrant in your territory

You want to have a minimum of three reasons to call back next Monday. Anything. Promise to drop off some literature, drop off a proposal, appointment, bring in a demo, whatever — don't worry about making those sales right off in a new territory. You're going to be getting your name around and that's going to make you money in the future.

I'll tell you, I don't know how many times one of my junior salesmen says, "I worked all day, made 50 calls, and it was a horrible day." Now, how could you make 50 calls and ask intelligent questions and have a horrible day? You've got to have a callback, a comeback, a lead, a name, or — I mean, you've got to have something. With IBM, they had a book that we used to keep; we didn't have to turn it in, it was for our own benefit. Like the Day Planners. If I went out and made ten calls, I'd have at least four places to come back to with an appointment or a demo or to see somebody or — I'd have something planned.

Whether you're having a good month or a bad one, your schedule is your rhythm

Be consistent. Be in each portion of your territory on the same day. It will help people in your quadrants get to know who you are. And when they know who you are, they'll begin to like you. And when they like you, they will buy. I worked on Monday, Tuesday, Wednesday, Thursday. Monday was ZIP code 304, Tuesday was 305, Wednesday was 306. Friday was my runaround day. Callback day for pickup, collect, you know, handle all the problems. So if I was in a sheriff's office on Monday, she says, "Well, he's busy. Can you come back?"

I'd say, "I'll come back next Monday, because I won't be back here till next Monday."

And so I got in that habit — even when I was with World Book. When I'd see somebody, and they'd say, "Oh, my husband's not home. Can you come back?"

I'd say, "Yeah, I can come back Tuesday, the 23rd, because that's the only day I'm over here."

And after you make that little old town once a week for four or five weeks, you get to know some people. And you cement a relationship with one or two, and you get a pretty good reputation, and you live off of that.

I wanted to be known as the IBM Man, same with World Book. And you couldn't go to a store and get IBM anywhere. Only place you could get IBM was me. I used to tell these people, "When I come in and represent IBM, and when you sign that order, then I represent you. When I go back to IBM, I'll represent you. And if you have any problems, you let me know."

There's value in a no-go sale

Part of the salesman's job — and they never do realize it — is not necessarily looking for the good prospect. It's eliminating the bad ones — and keeping a log of people who are not prospects today but might be tomorrow.

Being a good salesman means you make yourself the first line of defense for your customers

I represent my company when I come in to see you. Once you sign an order, I'm going to represent you when I go back to the company. Any problems, you call me.

You need to embrace any and all customers

Be creative. Being consistent in your ground game will open up new opportunities. Nothing is too big or too small. Not even a death row in a Florida prison. We had a prison down there, and I used to go back there on the death row and, man, that was a good territory. They were a good customer of mine. Hell, I'll bet I sold them ten typewriters.

I never will forget, there was a young boy. He was a great guy. Young kid, good-looking, you know, drove a Corvette. He went to work with me one day, and I took him down to that prison. And we had to go back through death row. I mean, we had to go back with two people with us. Man, these guys are yelling and whistling at him and trying to grab him. Embarrassed the hell out of me.

But I'll tell you what I used to do. They raised their own cattle, their own vegetables and everything. When I was working that territory, I'd arrive at that prison at 12 o'clock because at the cafeteria, you'd get a big steak for a buck. And the prisoners are serving it to you, and it was great. Used to do it all the time. I was making calls there, anyway. They were a good customer, a very good customer. They were the biggest employer down there, just a little old city, called Rayford, Rayford Prison. I mean, it was the only thing there. There was a little old service station, and I don't even think they had a bank.

I don't remember what they had. I just remember the prison. I mean, they probably bought 10 or 12 typewriters from me over a three-year period. You know, three or four a year. For that boondock territory, that was selling big. Point is, people overlook opportunities because they think it's beneath them. If you're out in the middle of nowhere, and that's the only thing around that looks like civilization, what are you going to do? You better call there.

And I'll tell you, I used to go through the metal detector and have to take the belt off and everything, and hold my hands up, and they'd search you. It was cool. Hell, I was 23 years old. I loved it.

And, every once in a while, on television, I'd see death row inmates, and Rayford was a real hot place down there. And I think, hey, there's old Bobby Gene. I remember him, in cell 32.

If death row can be a customer, so can anyone

With IBM, with Toshiba — any company without a copy machine was a prospect or potential prospect later on. And if they don't have a copy machine, maybe they didn't have a fax machine.

What are some internal problems salespeople have?

Instead of looking for leads in the newspaper or in a file somewhere, you've got to hit the pavement right now. Having too many customers can be a problem too, paralyzing. But either way, you have to start calling. A salesman needs to understand how many calls he needs to make to make the money he wants. It's math. If 10% of your calls result in a sale and you need 10 sales you need to make 100 calls. That's a fact. But you can't make calls while you're having coffee or getting a tan.

You know, when you're talking about a new salesman, that is their biggest challenge. They come out, and they're overwhelmed. "Where do I start? How do I get started? Who do I see first? Where do I go first?" That's what keeps them from making the call.

But it's really masking fear. Fear of rejection. So they don't start making calls. They do planning and they fidget with their leads. One of the benefits the salespeople have is the freedom of time. That can cut both ways. A salesman pops in, it's nine o'clock. "Well, I'll get some coffee, go get a haircut, and I figure I've got to make so many calls.

But the new salesman doesn't know how to organize his time. He doesn't know how to set priorities. So what's he doing? We used to call it salesman solitary. He's sitting there alone, going through call-backs, you know. Over at a coffee shop, you see a salesman, flipping through a book or file cards or a pile of business cards or something. That's his idea of callbacks. And he's looking for a hot one. Looking for a hot one. Not that any of them are. Unless you qualified them. They're false hope, but I'll tell you more about them later. But it's a disguise.

The truth is he doesn't want to go to work. He just wants to go make a sale but he doesn't know where to go. Salesman solitary. That's the reason movie houses used to open up at nine o'clock in the morning, during a school day. It's for salesmen. They're afraid to make calls. They can go to the air-conditioned movie. Salesman solitary.

Instead of looking for leads, you've got to hit the pavement right now

Well, let me give you an example. They hired me in Cape Canaveral. Wasn't there but a short time till they sent me to Tampa. I didn't know where I was. Never been to Tampa before in my life. But I made a living there inside of six months. Sent me to Jacksonville. I had been there before, so I knew the town but it had been a while. But, hell, I went out there and sold like crazy. Then they sent me up to Boston. I'd never been in Boston in my life. Solution? Just start selling. Solves all the problems. Go out knocking on doors.

I'll give you a story. I was coming in as a supervisor, back then, in Boston. And they were the worst branch in the United States. So I went in to meet the branch manager, who was leaving. He was getting fired. And I came in. 'Course, I had the suitcase and everything in my car, and he was going to take me out to get a hotel, and all this stuff. And I'm sitting there, and this gal came in, and she was in this management training program. And he introduced me to her, and, "Hi, how are you?"

"Fine."

She said, "Well, I hear you're going to work with us. That right?"

And I said, "Yeah, I'll be up here. And I'll be up here the next year, really."

And she said, "Well, when could you work with me?"

I said, "Well, Dear, anytime you want to."

"Well, how about right now?"

I said, "Well, fine. I'm not doing anything. Sure, let's go."

So we go out and get in the car. She looked at me and said, "Where do you want to go?"

26

"Well, I just got off the plane. I mean, I don't even know where I'm at, much less where I want to go. You tell me where we want to go."

She says, "I got a name a little up north of here."

And I said, "Okay, let's go."

So we drive, and we drive, and drive. We're talking. I said, "Well, let me ask you something. I love to see the outskirts of Boston, here, but we've been traveling for 25 minutes. How much further is it?"

She says, "Oh, about another half hour."

I said, "Now, wait a minute. Wait a minute. Why are we going up there?"

She says, "Well, I've got a name."

And I said, "Well, that's fine. And what else do you have?"

She says, "Well, I've got the address."

And I said, "Well, that's fine. What else?"

She says, "Well, I know they have kids."

I said, "Well, that's good. What are the kids' names?"

"Well, I don't know."

I said, "Well, how are they doing in school?"

She said, "I don't know."

I said, "Is the mother home?"

She said, "Well, I don't know."

I said, "Well, look. We just passed about a hundred mailboxes, and I see a gym set and a ball on a lawn and a — you know, there's a tricycle right here. And there's their name and address, right on the mailbox. How is your name any better than these last hundred?"

She said, "Well, I don't know."

I said, "Well, there's a lady out there, standing in the driveway. Why don't we pull in and see her?"

She said, "Well, I don't know her."

I said, "Heck, park this thing, and I'll introduce you." So we went in, wrote the damned thing up, right there on the spot, and spent the rest of the day in that neighborhood. I don't think we got another order, but we got one order. It was so funny. Just do it. I said, "Hell, I don't need any more driving. Let's go talk to somebody."

Defer to people's sense of dignity

There's a fine line though. See, I had a lot of teachers as salesmen, and we never asked them to call on their own students, but many of them did, though that was not a requirement. You know, if they did, they did, and if they didn't, we didn't care. But a teacher could speak with authority. And a mother would listen to a teacher, just like a doctor recommending an aspirin. But they wouldn't go out and put themselves in a demeaning or an embarrassing position unless they believed in the product.

If you do everything right, the money will start walking in without your effort

I had my own prospects calling me to give me tips. Half of them, I couldn't even remember who they were. But at IBM we used to really cement a relationship with the secretary, because they were the ones that used the equipment. And they are the ones that whine and complain if the equipment is not up to snuff. I don't know how many times we'd come in, on purpose, and see a head secretary and say, "You know, they're getting a new typewriter for that girl over there, and you're on that piece of junk — you'd better talk to your boss and go in and raise hell." You talk about an easy sell. I mean, the guy, the boss just calls me in. "Hey, we need another typewriter." We called it bluebird. But we'd come in and we'd shake up the homeostasis. We'd try to make them dissatisfied with what they had. Thing is, the secretary was very happy because she was typing on the latest, greatest thing.

That makes you a friend. I used to have secretaries calling me. "Jim, you know, there's an Underwood salesman or Royal salesman, who brought a machine in. I don't know where it's going. It's upstairs. You'd better get down here."

But people, today, I don't think they could make a living without a name, lead, or referral. They don't want to go out and work. They're always looking for the shortcut to get to a sale. It's the old adage, "Give me some heat, and I'll cut you some wood." It doesn't work that way. You've got to get out and do the grunt work, cut the firewood. I'll tell you one thing, when orders start coming to you, you're catching "Bluebirds." It's the order — it just falls across the transom. You know, you don't even work for it, somebody calls you up and says, "Hey, I'm ready to order another one." That was the secret of working a territory. You get a big insurance company that's standardized on your equipment. Once you got that done, heck, I'd just send out purchase orders. You don't have to work them at all. You'd just make a phone call at the end of the month. "Hey, Bob! I've got end of the month coming up. Working on a trip. Need anything?"

"Yeah, I'm going to hire three people."

"Well, let me get you three more machines." Bluebirds.

If you got the senior territory — the insurance companies and the riders and the hospitals — and, I mean, the phone just rang, and you just — they had the bluebirds falling into place.

The customer base is enormous. You need to hit them surgically and systemically to see the full range of opportunities

Territories are huge. But at the end of the day — keep it simple. Start next door and work your way out. The last person you think of? The one right next door. You know the neighbor. You know you're going to get in. They've got kids. Why don't you go next door?

"Oh, I never thought of that."

That's the first thing I did when I worked somewhere.

See, every time I'd go to meet one of these part-timers to work with — no matter, Jacksonville and Boston and Ohio — they'd say, "Well, I'll meet you down at the coffee shop."

I'd say, "Well, I don't want to meet at the coffee shop. Why don't I just pick you up at your house?"

"Oh, okay. Well, where do you want to go?"

I say, "Well, I want to go next door."

"Oh, that's my neighbor."

"Well, that's the reason I want to go next door. I don't want to spend the whole day knocking on doors. I'd rather get in and talk to somebody. What about across the street?"

"Well, I don't know them."

"Well, come on. I'll introduce you to them. You're their neighbor, hell! They ought to know you. Think about it."

That's the thing. It's all about managing your territory and a good salesman starts at home and works outward. And he makes calls. It's that simple.

Chapter 3

The Approach: Think, Feel, React

People have a fear of going out. What do they fear? It's rejection, embarrassment — that's a good fear. A salesman needs to overcome fear at three points in a sale. How do you get over them? It's easy.

The three doors between you and an order

See, we're talking about three doors. Well, the first one is the *trap door* that's in your head. What keeps you from even wanting to go to work is the fear of failure, the fear of the put-off, the fear of embarrassment, fear of — whatever those imaginary fears are. That's what keeps you from making calls.

The second door is the *office door*. On this one you have a thousand reasons not to push it open. Here are some of them. So-and-so was going to call you back. He didn't call yesterday, but he might call this morning . . . I've got to talk to the sales manager . . . He can't make a decision without my input, and I've got to get the technician to get this set up. You've got a thousand reasons not to get out of the comfort zone and to that door. No rejection from doing nothing, right?

The third hardest door to get through is your *car door*. Not in your car. Out of your car. I mean, well, it's 20 below zero out there, and you've got the heater cranked up and a cup of coffee, and you're kind of, you know, checking that territory out and looking for that friendly door. That car door is a hard one to get through.

Or it's the middle of August, 110 in the shade, you've got that air conditioner kicking out there. You feel occupied when you're driving. You feel you're working. You're not productive, but in your mind you feel busy. I am scouting out that territory. Done it a thousand times before, but it needs one more sweep.

What's the answer? But if you have three places to go on Monday, you at least have three reasons to get through your door. It may not be that productive, but now you're in the territory, right? And your intention is to stay there all day. So those three things get you back and out the door.

Now before you go beat yourself up hitting the pavement, you should understand that there are some things that are out of your control.

Timing and luck

There is nothing called luck in our business. You could come in with three orders and a guy could say, "Well, hell, he's lucky." I don't think there's any luck to it at all. But timing's important. If I go into a house selling World Book, and the husband just got cut back on his hours, they're two months behind on their mortgage payment, and the kids are doing great — well, they're a great prospect, but the timing's horrible — as opposed to the neighbor, whose husband just got a promotion. These people are two payments ahead on their house but the kids are struggling in school. As to the first house, in another year, I can come back on these people, their situation and circumstances may have changed, so they're still be a good prospect. Do you see? It was timing, not luck. Timing is the important thing.

32

So you're ready to go. Hold your horses!

Before you pick up the phone, before you knock on any doors, it's time to do some homework. It's time to find out about your customer. It'll pay.

Before you knock on the door, let's start with a *precanvass*. It's how we familiarize ourselves to what's around us, what's going on. It's information gathering. Let's take the business I'm driving to see. I get to their office so I look around the parking lot. I can check the cars. I see the president drives a Jaguar, and the vice president drives a Mercedes convertible. Then I look in the back lot, and all these jacked-up cars with rifles in the back — pretty swinging group here, I think.

Conversely, we go into another type business and we see a four-door Lincoln, a four-door Cadillac, four-door Mercedes — very well, but kind of conservative tint. So I look at the building, the maintenance. Is the grass cut? Has the snow been removed? All those clues as to their values. It's just a feel. Am I dealing with a swinging group, or is this more of a conservative group? Do they have a private place for the president, or does he have to park on the street? The appearance of the building tells me something. How well maintained is it? Are they prosperous or are they pinching pennies? I get some of that in my precanvass, more if I get the quarterly report or stockholders' report or something in the newspaper to give me some background on the company.

Finally, I love to know their competitors before I even call on them. Love to know their competitors. When I was with IBM, I wanted to know a guy's competition inside and out. See, if I know his competition just bought a composing machine which was cold type versus the old hot type — linotype — and they were saving money and were getting the same quality and better production, I know that if he knew that his

33

competitor had just bought this machine, and he wants to compete with him, he might get my machine, which was even better. So I kind of like to know what the competition is when I'm calling on someone. Now, most of the time, I can't get it on a cold call. But if it's a vertical market, and I'm going to concentrate on it and make numerous calls, I want know the background before I even talk to anybody.

Learn everything you possibly can before you start pitching

Read whatever you can about the company. Do a drive-by and eye-ball the place. But don't let this change the core of your pitch. You're just getting into the mindset of your customer. You're getting a better idea of what their needs are, what they respond to, and how your product can bring value to them. Just get a feel of who and what you're dealing with. Your other instincts might be wrong. But you've got to start somewhere.

Use more than just your eyes

Collect intel from anyone in the neighborhood and use that to find the customer most likely to buy. I look at an old lady mowing her grass, or a guy cutting weeds, or something, and I'd go up and let my hair down. I'd say, "Hey, I'm Jim Murphy." I said, "I'm new here, and I really need some help. My boss told me I had to talk to 12 people who have kids. And I don't know where in the heck they are around here. Is that lady over —" and I'd point right there. "Does that lady over there have any kids?" There's a bicycle and a gym set and things over there.

"Yeah, she's got them."

And I said, "Well, what type of kids?"

"Well, hell, I don't know. They come over here, and they bug me, and — you know, go sell her some books."

"What about next to —"

"Naw, that's an old lady."

"What about down there?"

"Yeah, now, they've got two kids down there. They come up here and help me mow. They're the politest kids, and they're nice —"

And I'm making notes of this, so, when I go up, it was, "Who sent you?" and I have an answer. A neighbor.

If no one is there to tell you explicitly, just take a look around

A lot of times, I'd go in a neighborhood and I wouldn't see anybody, you know. I'd see signs. I'd see bicycles, tricycles, gym sets. So I'd pick the house with the tricycles and get started.

Now you're ready.

Pick up the phone. Knock on a door. You've got to get inside.

And nobody likes the humiliation of getting inside. Lots of sale reps were scared to death to go inside someone else's house. But there are ways.

It's pretty damn intimidating, as a new door-to-door salesman. No question. Scare you to death. The farmhouse was the worse, because you pull up there, there are no dogs — till you get out of your car. And then, from around the back, between you and the car, are the dogs.

You're coming in as a stranger, you know. And back then, it was kind of subterfuge. I mean, we never told them we were selling World Book. I mean, that was the last thing in the world you'd tell them. I never told anybody I was selling encyclopedias. I said, "I'm in education." You know, "I'm selling books," or reference material. We used all kinds of euphemisms. I might say, "I'm visiting mothers who have children in school. I found out from your neighbor that you have three kids up here in St. Agnes. Is that right? I came to see you about Bobby. Could I talk to you a few minutes? I've got to be brief."

I said, "I've got to be brief." That's open for interpretation, you know. But it was Field Enterprise standard verbiage. "We're Field Enterprise & Education, Incorporation and I must be brief."

I don't think we had any particular trick but, for the first three or four years, you'd bite your tongue off before you'd tell them you were with World Book. We used to say we were with Field Enterprises. But later on, the last four or five years I was with World Book, they had such a good name, that didn't hurt. Really didn't hurt.

Going into someone's house is not easy

Don't worry if you're nervous. It took me a long time to learn how to do that. It took me a little bit longer to feel comfortable doing it, because I felt I came in under a subterfuge, and as soon as they found out I'm selling World Book, they're going to kick me out — never happened. Never happened.

Knock on the door

"Hi, I'm Jim Murphy. I've been talking to some of the neighbors around here, and I understand you have some kids in school. Is that true? Good. I came by to visit with you. I want to talk to you about your child. Could I come in and see you a few minutes?"

"What about?"

"Well, we're talking about what they can do in school and what you can do in the home to help them achieve in school. I'm sure you'd want to know more about it, wouldn't you?"

"Well, I'm busy."

"I'll be brief." I keep looking at my watch. "I'll be brief."

Never put my foot in the door. Never. What I'd do is knock on the door. When they came, I would try to step back, anticipating and drawing them out. Well, everybody's got space. But, as you have the tendency to step back, many will come out. And that's a good sign that, you know, that they're a friendly person. But what I wanted to do is get in.

Many will either refuse you to enter or just not open the door. I'd say for every one I got in, maybe seven I didn't. It takes perseverance.

You'll get in some of the damndest ways if you're clever

When I was a young salesperson, often you walk up to the house or the office, and there's a giant sign that says, "Absolutely no soliciting." Heck, that's a welcome sign. The husband put it up, it ain't the wife. I go up there and knock right on the door. But as soon as they come to the door, I say, "I'm terribly sorry." I said, "I walked up here, and I didn't see the sign till the last minute, so I knocked on the door, and I thought that it would not be correct for me to turn around and leave. So, while I'm here, could I talk to you? I'll be brief." Yep, you always say, "While I'm here, I'll be brief."

A lot of times, we'd go up and see a For Sale sign that would say SOLD on it. New people moved in. I'd say, "Hi, Doug, I'm Jim Murphy. I want to welcome you to the neighborhood. Could I see you a few minutes?" If you're brand new in the neighborhood, you don't care.

Or maybe someone will be right there on the lawn.

I remember one — there's a story. There was a guy out there, raking his leaves. And this salesman was telling me about it. He said, "Well, the hardest part is getting the rake out of the guy's hand and get him in the house. That's the tough part." So he started talking and the guy's resisting. And he finally did something he didn't like to do: He told the guy that he was selling books. In fact, he told him he was selling World Book.

The man with the rake said, "You know, my wife and I talked about that, and we intend to get a set of those one day," he said, "but can't do it right now."

Frank said, "Why not?"

He said, "Well, we don't have any place to put them."

He said he looked back at his three-story house. He said, "Well, you're an optometrist. If I went up to you, and you told me I needed glasses, and I told you I didn't have any place to put them, what would you tell me?" So they both started laughing and joking and got friendly, and he went in and sold the books.

The basics work anywhere — just pay attention

When I was selling IBM, the hardest person to see was the doctor. And out in the waiting room they had the sliding glass windows back then, and the receptionist was the bulldog. Got to get past the secretary. The hardest thing was getting into the back and seeing the doctor.

I could generally do it by asking for help. If anybody ever calls you and asks you for help, what do you say? "What can I do for you?" Right, well, I mean, that's the way we'd start. I remember selling the pathologist down at St. Luke's Hospital. I sold him one of our machines. And the reason I remember it, because, when I sold it, I had to go back and deliver it.

It came in, and I went by to see him, and the secretary said, "Yeah, he's down in the laboratory. You can go see him." So I went down there. Well, I had also sold him a suspended microphone and he's working the foot pedal, dictating as he worked, knowing his words would come out on the typewriter in the back here. And I remember walking up there and saying, "Hey, Doc! How you doing?" I looked down, and there was somebody's heart in his hands. I almost threw up.

Think, feel, react

You don't go in selling. You go in talking about the thing that's most important to your prospect, and that's their kids. And you can look around a house pretty quick and tell they're proud of their kids. If you see books around, and magazines, and things like that, you get a feel for the sort of parents living there. Is education important to them? If it looks like their prized possession is a kewpie doll dad won at the carnival last week, I'm not going to spring on them Shakespeare and Monet, or anything like that.

But up in New England, there's a lot of educated, cultured people there. And you go in, and you can just see their library and their records and their music and their books, and the old man is sitting there with a slide rule, well, you know you're in an educated home. And you wouldn't talk about stuff that you'd talk about in South Georgia.

Memorize sweep cards

Let me ask you. The governor is coming over to visit you and he's bringing a couple of dignitaries, so where are you going to entertain them? In the living room. Now, your brother-in-law and a cousin and a couple of guys are going to come over and just shoot the bull, where are you going to entertain them? In my kitchen or entertainment area.

Okay. I like to be in the kitchen or the entertainment area. But I want to go through the living room to sweep it, because if I see a Picasso or a fake Rembrandt and look at the table and they've got an Oxford English Dictionary, and I hear some type of classical music, I know they appreciate education for the value of education. But I want to get back to the kitchen, because I want to sweep that refrigerator's door full of pictures, too.

See, if I'd go in the house, and I'd see a pickup truck with a $300 shotgun in the back window and $800 worth of oversized tires and a set of $800 golf clubs rotting and rusting in the driveway, with a $500 riding mower sitting in the back yard rusting, I know they can afford whatever they want.

Focus your pitch on adding value associated with your customer's problems

You need to convince them that your product will solve their problems. In the beginning, you've got to forget your products, forget your company, forget your commission check, and think of their problems. Because they are not going to buy your product because it's glitzy. They're going to buy what's going to solve their problem.

Now, how do you know it's going to solve their problem till you ask them? The best thing to do is start with the end user and find out what the problem is. Then, you can magnify it and exaggerate it. When you get to the boss you've already got partial agreement. The boss knew these problems existed, but they weren't all channelized into one little thing.

What type of questions would you ask a thousand different prospects? See, like "can't afford" comes disguised a thousand different ways. But if you analyze it, it's still "can't afford." So you probably have key questions you ask a prospect to find out if there's a need for your product. What are those key questions? Now, you can disguise them any way you want, but basically, what is the key problem? The answer will be the information you need so you can think how your product is going to solve that problem.

If the prospect allows you to continue, it shows there's some interest, or he wouldn't allow you to continue. But there's not enough to make a financial decision. He has an interest; doesn't want to get rid of you yet. Wants to hear a little bit more. "But I ain't buying." Okay, fine. I understand that. But, if he knew what you knew, he'd buy right away. Therefore, you've got to show him more.

Do your research

Do your recon so that you can find your *real* end user at the company. Let's say I'm calling on a company to sell a forklift. I don't want to go in the front door and get a set of glasses, a name tag, and sign in, and all that bull — I don't want that. I'd prefer to catch the janitor and compliment him on how nice the building looks, and how he must be wonderfully appreciated here, and la-dee-dah. And, by the way, I'd say, "You know a forklift operator in there?"

He'd say, "Joe."

"Oh, can you take me in the back and introduce him to me? I'd like to talk to him." I don't want to go in the front door. I want to talk to the operator. He's using the equipment. So then I'll come up and compliment him. "Gee, I understand you keep this place going. I understand, if it wasn't for you and your dedication, that the whole place would shut down."

So I jack with him a little bit. And then I say, "Well, let me ask you something. If you were going to design your own forklift, what would be the one or two things you'd change?

"Oh, they've got that emergency brake right in the middle, and it should be over here, on the right."

41

And I'd say, "Now, if you were going to design one, how would you do it?"

"Well, I'd make sure that the hydraulics do this and did that when I move the boom."

"And I'd say, well, let me ask you something. If we could get you a new machine in here, just like you wanted it — just like you want it — who would be the man that would influence that decision?" This guy doesn't care about cost. He ain't paying for it.

"Well, you ought to see the warehouse manager. That's the boss's brother-in-law, and he can get anything he wants."

"Well, if he increased production back here, would he get a raise?"

"Well, I'm sure he would."

"Well, introduce me to him."

So he'll take me up.

I get there and say, "Hey, I understand you're in charge of this whole operation back here, and it's really got a problem. Joe says every time he uses the hydraulics on the forklift with that boom, them barrels shake, and he's scared to death they're going to fall out and hurt somebody — got a lawsuit here. And if you could get a new machine in here, he said he could do everything faster, save money, cut lost barrels.

"Yeah, we've had all kind of problems. Well, if we can get this stuff off those big trucks, before they leave here at 3 o'clock, that would help because they don't come back until the next day."

"Well, I don't want you to say anything to your boss, but I'd like for you to tell me, in front of your boss, what the problems are, and I could put you a machine in here for nothing — not going to cost him anything. But don't tell him that."

"What are you talking about?"

I keep him in the dark, but I want him to introduce me to Mr. Big. And I want him, also, to kind of embellish the problems we've got in the back room. Then he can leave.

Okay, we get the forklift operator to introduce us to the warehouse manager, and he always wants to increase production. So once he understands the problem and introduces the problem to me, then I'd like him to introduce me to the key influencer. He can't make the decision, but he can sure push it. That's who I want to be in my corner. Then the demo or the presentation or whatever you're doing. That's the next big step.

Once we've got the Influencer in front of the Wallet, we've married the end-user to the money

This is the same as finding the child and pairing him/her with the mother/father.

Now, we're working on the problem, and I never talk solutions. "We understand we've increased production. Jones Plastics did this, and they did that, and they cut their production. Now, I don't know if you can do that or not, but if — if — if —" and you bring that "if" along and try either to go sell something on the spot or set up an appointment to come back with a proposal. "I don't want you to take my word for anything, but I want to put a machine back here, in the back, for three days — no obligation; not going to cost you a penny. And if it will do what I say it will do, I don't expect you to buy it, but if I could give it to you, place it in here with no cash on your part, would you have an interest in it?"

"Well, if it'll do what you say it'll do . . . ." Equipment will sell itself. Same with World Book. We had a three-day think-it-over clause. I put them out there on trial. "Three days, think it over. You don't have to buy. Don't want it, send it back." So when you have a product that you believe in, which I do with IBM, and I certainly do with World Book, and I believe in Toshiba — put it in on a trial. It will sell itself. It's new. It smells good. It's not broken or patched up. The pages are crisp. The pictures are colorful. You'll never take it back.

Chapter 4

SATMAC: The Canned Talk

You've got to develop an iron-clad, memorized, and canned talk that you know works — that you could put your own personal money on. If people follow this exactly, to ten different prospects, I guarantee you 1 out of 10 will buy. That's how good, how tested it has to be.

You have to have a canned talk. I think that is absolutely a must. Everybody resisted when I told them that. "Have you ever seen Ed McMahon get out there, on television, and pitch Budweiser? You think Budweiser said, 'Ed, you're so good, just go say whatever you want to say?' I guarantee, he practiced that thing a hundred times."

I used to make the comparison — you remember when you were in high school? The kid in the play was standing there and saying, "Well, er, uh, uh —"? He didn't memorize it. But you see a professional actor, I don't care if there was a fire in the theater, he doesn't miss a line. He just keeps going right on. He responds to the audience. He can respond to the audience because it's memorized and rehearsed. But a kid who didn't memorize is scared to death. So a canned presentation is mandatory. You make five presentations of the same product to five different people, it's going to end up being canned anyway, you know.

The most important reason for having a canned talk — so you can listen

There's the real truth about it all. You can start concentrating on their responses, their excuses, start developing the clinchers you're going to use, ways to overcome their excuses, their objections, which you know are coming. So by knowing your pitch like it was second nature you can focus on listening to your customers and watching out for those subtle tell signs that let you know what objections you need to overcome. The three flippant, most-used excuses are: "Can't afford," "Buy later," and "I have to see someone." In the book business, the most frequent was, "I have to see my husband." They wanted me to think it was real. But it was not real. So I kept on. If I had been a newlywed, I'd probably buy that. But I'd been married. So I don't buy that. They will buy from you.

The basic message of the canned talk is that you're not going to take the most common excuses

They become disguised in a hundred different ways, but if you back them out and analyze them, break them down, it will always come down to "can't afford," "buy later" — I mean, they may say it different ways, but that's basically what they're telling you.

Never make an appointment — come in cold

If you have an appointment, and they know in advance you're coming, and they know you're a salesman, they have their resistance built up. What I shoot for is an unprejudiced person. I don't want them to like me, and I don't want them to dislike me. I just want them to be neutral.

Let's start on the need analysis. "Let's talk about what you need, and let me see what I can do. I don't know if I can help you or not, but what if and what if —" By questioning people, you can come pretty quickly to the conclusion that either they're qualified or not qualified. And that's really what you're searching for.

Locate the problem

The beginning of your canned talk is always designed to find out what problem your prospect has so you can convince him your product will solve it.

Find out what their problems are. And once we uncover a problem, then I feel my job is to exaggerate that problem, make them so aware that they have one that they develop an overwhelming need to solve it. And only where I get him to believe he really he has a problem can I show him a solution.

"Oh, that damned judge. He sends me over, he wants nine copies of everything. And five are good, and the other — well, we've got to type it twice."

"Well, you've got a real problem here. You're paying that girl and she's got to do it twice? And now the judge is holed up, and his time is valuable. Suppose there's a way you could do ten copies, and the tenth copy was just as clear as the second one. Would that have any interest to you?"

Take out your order pad right away so you won't spook them with it later on

The order pad has the price right there in bold print, fully in the open. I've always negotiated with an order pad out — never a yellow pad — it's the first thing that comes out; it's right there, price and all. Then, as we talk, I make notes on the order pad. When they'd tell me the kids' names, I'd write them down. You know, you make eight or ten calls today and hear 40 different names, you're calling Bobby, Sam, and Susan. Because I don't want to wait till the last minute to reach in my briefcase and pull out an order pad. It's on the table before I do anything, and I use it as a scratch pad. But see, we're negotiating all the time. And my first close, always, is not a close. It's a test. And I always write down the total price, knowing what you're going to say before I write it down. Because the first excuse is always the same. "I can't do anything like that right now," you know. So that's not a close. I'm trying to test — there's a will to resist and a will to persist, and I've got to get that first excuse off the table. We call that SATMAC. You Smile, Agree, Turn the excuse, show More value, And Close. SATMAC. Smile. Agree. Turn the excuse, show More value. And Close again.

The first step of SATMAC — always diffuse a price objection

Objecting to the price of the encyclopedia is automatic, it's a Pavlovian, off-the-cuff response. Everybody's going to do it. So, I've just got to allow you to get that off your chest, or we ain't going to go anywhere. I can understand the old think/thank/thought. "That's exactly what I thought the first time I saw that, Mr. Joe. But the more I thought about it, and a friend explained it to me, now I could see where it was really the most valuable thing I ever did." And then, what people don't do anymore is, on every close, you show a fact, turn it to a benefit. All salespeople do that, but they never clinch it. A clinch is, "Wouldn't you agree?" "Isn't that so?" "You've found that to be true?" "Wouldn't that be helpful?" "Don't you agree?"

Agree, right?

So they say, "Well, I can't afford anything like that."

And they don't know it, but I'm not going to try to sell it to you, anyway. I'm ready to spring my second close. I'm going to lease it to you — 12 bucks a month, 18 a month, 40, whatever it is. But I've got to let you get all that off your chest first. Then I'm going to show more value, play your excuse down.

"Well, I can understand where you came from. That's exactly what I thought, the first time I saw that. But let me show you one more thing, because you did mention that your secretary, over there, is getting a little frustrated. We have a particular machine, over here, that not only relaxes her hand — increases her speed — but relaxes her endurance because we can set the pressure on each key to make it suitable to whatever she wants to do. So it's a real benefit for her. But don't worry about that. Let me show you one other quick thing here." Then you go back and show them more material. Now we're talking about increasing your gross productivity, making her job a little more comfortable and easier on her, taking the grunt out of her work, keeping her from snapping at you, and we're keeping the judge happy. "Would that be worth 12 bucks a week? Forty a month?"

Now I'm comparing benefits for the price. You have to mentally work that out. That's the value of a memorized presentation. Once it's memorized, you don't have to grope for what you're going to say, you know what you're going to say. Now you can concentrate on what the prospect says, which is going to be the determining factor.

Canned — memorized. Even if you don't, if you went out, and you were selling fountain pens, after ten presentations, it's canned, anyway. Full timers, we'd make them memorize that thing. Now you can be more conscious of excuses and build the need, and overcome excuses. And you can remember things that they're telling you.

Do lots of calls

I'd say five calls in the morning and five in the afternoon, easy. Fifty a week. Yeah, but that wasn't a magic number, or anything, because some weeks we'd only make 20 and have 10 sales. Other weeks, we'd make 80 calls and have 2 sales. I'd say, on the average, I did ten a day — ten a day.

Rejection is part of the game but it's over-played

No one is going to throw you out. I'll bet I've been in ten thousand houses, and I can only remember two I was invited out. One of them, I had a young kid with me, and I was trying to impress him how to close, and they weren't even good prospects, and I was really putting some heat on. And that guy said, "Wait a minute. Excuse me." Went out in the kitchen, called his wife in there, and they're in there having an argument.

I told the kid, I said, "This doesn't sound too good."

So they both came out, and they wouldn't sit down. "We've had enough. You've had enough. Your time's up. There's the door. Don't come back!" That embarrassed the hell out of me. But, I'm telling you, out of 10,000 houses, I'll bet you 9,000 of them, if I got an order or not, I could get back in. I could get back in. I guarantee you I could.

And then, the other one, I was training another young kid, and it was raining that day, in Jacksonville. And I had a raincoat on. I think I had a hat. And we went up there, and the lady came to the door — an African-American lady. She said, "What? What?"

And I said, "Well, I have to come in to see the kids." You know, I was speaking with some authority.

And all of a sudden, I heard doors slamming, the commode's flushing, and the windows opened. I didn't know what the hell was going on. She said, "Well, come on in."

Well, I'm sitting there, demonstrating, you know. She isn't paying any more attention than the man in the moon. It was a dope house. They weren't common in those years but I was right in the middle of one.

The pitch is more than talk — it's about demos and props

At IBM, I had nine demos. I had nine demonstrators, and my job was to get them out on trial and come back and close before the end of the month. I had to turn them, because I had a quota. When I started, it was 10 or so typewriters. When I left, it was twice that. Only had eight or nine demonstrators, so you had to turn them. Drop them off, come back, close a sale, take them to another business and repeat it all again.

Always use visuals

For example, I used to carry around a K–12 curriculum guide for World Book pitches. It's a little booklet, a national curriculum guide. And it shows the third grade. In the third grade they study pioneers and patriots, and the human body, or they're studying flowers. And it's from K to 12, the whole national curriculum for what people should be studying at each grade level.

That's what I used for my warm-up. "Now, you, as a father, with a kid in the fourth grade, I can show you what they're studying in school — or close to what they're studying. And, would it be helpful if you knew what he was going to study next year, especially in the summer, to get prepared for fourth grade?"

Oh, it was my bible. It was my bible.

Now, what they did nationally, I don't know. But, man! I carried around that national curriculum. How you going to demonstrate World Book without something to show them? You need visuals.

Your canned talk needs to match your canned visuals

I'd open my World Book and turn to a page. "Yeah, wouldn't this be helpful? Could you see, when your little girl's studying biology, you could have used that acetate on the human body? Do you see, when you were back in fifth grade, how these pictures would have helped?" So it's the visuals that keep them occupied to get you clinching, clinching, clinching.

All of this is trying just to obliterate that money thing. That's no big deal. Money is no object.

Specific visuals are a necessity

Stay moving, fluid. Bring value closer. Definitely at World Book, yes. And with Toshiba, we always carried literature and had some type of a visual presentation.

When I'm summing up and talking to the man about ordering it, better let him see what he's ordering, right? He ought to know what it is and get some agreement: "This will be helpful. This will solve that problem. And you'd agree with that, wouldn't you?" If I'm going for the order, I need to do that. So, yeah, some type of visual is imperative.

Visuals sell. If you don't believe it, look at some of these infomercials on television. I remember Culligan Water called on me when Jimmy was four years old, back in 1968. Never forget the presentation. I don't remember the guy's name, but I'll never forget the presentation. You know, the box, about that big. And he pulled corroded water pipes out and test tubes and vials — I never imagined. He had test tubes and vials and he had a crooked pipe and had a smock he put on. And I was just amazed at all this crap he got out of this little box.

But his demonstration. It was just the visuals. He was very articulate and, I mean, it was a great presentation. In Florida, you had hard water.

And he'd show you all that corrosion built up in here. And he took a coffee pot with a ring around it and put this plain water, wiped it out. I mean, I was impressed. I told the guy, "You sold me on soft water." I mean, it's horrible in Florida.

Be creative — think outside the box

It's okay to go outside the manual, or as I called it — "the Bible." But the nice thing was, at IBM, on the type bar machine, I could go in the engineering department, if you wanted special keys. I'd let the secretary pick out the keys she wanted or where she wanted them. We could set the impression for her touch. And we'd convince her this machine was manufactured just for her specs. "What do you want? What do you like?" You know, get her building her own typewriter, which is getting her to the close.

Use standard services of your company as value-added parts of your pitch.

I sometimes had to be creative in ways the marketing department wasn't ready to sign off on yet at IBM. Like when I sold a tape recorder and a dictating machine, I packaged them together as a "word processor." The canned talk allowed us to be creative, to adapt. I called it "word processing." And I believe I'm the first one in the United States to use that. So my boss loved it. And I sold the first two magnetic tape machines — the forerunners of the storage typewriter, about the size of a secretary's desk, and two mag tapes. You could put names and addresses on this side of a letter, here, and merge them. That was a big deal back then.

Here's the way it was and could be. You'd dictate it to a secretary who types it, brings it back to you, you rephrase it, cross out, make some corrections. Suppose there was a way — and I'd pull out my little dictating machine — you could talk into this, and it would automatically come out, typed on the outside, error free? How would you like that?

Wow! I sold tons of those big machines — they were $10,000-dollar machines. So my boss called the district manager. "Come on down and go to work for the hot-shot salesman." So we go out, and I'm calling on Alton Box Company. I remember, right there, in Jacksonville, the St. John's River, making this fabulous presentation. He's just sitting there.

And we walked back to the car, and he said, "Murphy, you're going to get your ass fired." He said, "I got to go talk to your boss. You cannot use that word 'word processing.' Get that off that flipchart. And they cannot talk on that and have it come out automatically typed. They got to take it out and —"

I said, "Tom, we have a wire that'll run from our machine, out to a transcriber — all through the walls, back upstairs, downstairs. They can sit there and type on an MTST. Once it's typed, all they do is put in a name and address for tomorrow."

"Yeah, but you can't use that." So they wrote me — they were going to fire me, or something. Of course nothing happened. But I sold a ton of equipment that way.

When engineering, marketing, and legal aren't on your side, you need to turn to God for help in your talk

Be observant. Be seeing what's going on. You know, if they've got a bible on the table, they're probably down in the heart, and we've got to hold their hands and pray about this, you know. You've got to observe the situation you're in. I've prayed with many people.

All these ultra-religious Pentecostal people: "I can't do it without the Lord."

"Well, I feel the same way. Let's talk about that." We'll hold hands and pray. "Yeah, the Lord's telling me you ought to do it."

People are funny.

Family dynamics are also cues to look for when making a sale

As with before, nothing is sacred. At World Book, if I ran into a divorced woman that had a pretty good job, she had two kids, she — especially if they're boys — she didn't have a chance. You know, there's certain things little boys want to know about themselves and their body, and they don't feel comfortable going to the mother. If you had a choice, you'd let them pick it up in the street or, if you had good material here, written by, you know, experts — may not be the most beneficial thing in the world, but it wouldn't hurt, would it?

After the sale is done and the order form is signed, the pitch still isn't done

The pitch needs to also include an "ask" for referrals. Trinkets and service calls are the best ways to do this. Offer them choice. But understand that the presentation isn't done at "yes." You want to get some fresh leads. We had great giveaways. We had a world globe — it would spin — and a Bible and an atlas. We'd give them out for referrals. Kids loved those globes. Now, a lot of people would tighten it up. I'd only give it to you if you bought from me. I mean, if you give me ten names, I guaran-damn-tee I'll sell two or three — I guarantee you I will. And the service calls after the sale were very, very successful for the many people who used it. Now, salesmen that were too busy to make the service call, they didn't have places to go. The ones who made the service call always had a place to go — they were going back to a satisfied customer, and oh-by-the-way, they'd get three new referrals and give out a globe.

Now, a lot of people were tough and said, "Make me three appointments, and I'll give you a Bible." I like that one even better than the ten names. "You make me three appointments, and I'll give you —" whatever it is. And these salespeople would do that if they bought or not. Now, it was ingrained, and I knew it for a fact for 22 years, I don't care what a stubble-bumbler we had, if they went through a company presentation, guaranteed, one out of five. One out of five would buy.

But at the end of the day, the canned talk is only as good as how many times you give it. *You have to pitch enough times to let the law of averages swing in your favor.* That's when you make money. Yeah, that law of averages I think is so important in selling people on selling. Selling is hard, but it pays if you put in the work. Going down the street, cold. Blip, blip, blip, blip, blip. If you call on a prospect and give a company presentation, the way I ran our Toshiba company, it's a *guarantee of a thousand dollars for so many presentations, regardless of orders* or not. I would guarantee my sales force 1,000 dollars if they'd make 100 full presentations. With a commission of 100 bucks they only needed to make 10 sales and I wouldn't pay a dime. But if they made a hundred presentations and they didn't make 10 sales, I'd pay the difference.

That bet will work because commission works with the same certainty as salary. You need to look at it as the same compensation that everyone else has if they get paid on the 15th and 30th. But people get scared of commission. "Well, I don't like commission." Let me tie one thing into that objection, which was put in my head a long time ago.

A guy said, "Well, I don't like commission sales because, you know, it's so unreliable, getting paid and all."

I said, "Well, let me ask you something. If you went to work for Joe Blow down there, at five dollars an hour, and you worked real, real hard, I mean, even overtime three days a week, would you get paid? No. Well, let's say you worked a whole week. Would you get paid? No, you wouldn't, either. If you worked nine days, you wouldn't get paid. You've got to put in two weeks."

Selling is not taught, it's caught

Well, it's the same thing with selling. You've got to put in the number of presentations. You've got to put in the number of hours and the number of calls. And we would convert it from hours into number of calls, number of presentations, number of orders, and put out a guarantee on it.

Now, most people wouldn't follow it. But the ones who did were successful. Guaranteed. Fifty a week, ten a day. It's hard work. And you just catch on, but you've got to make a bunch of calls to do it. You've got to get a bunch of calls, get a bunch of rejections, get a bunch of put-downs before you really know what you're doing.

Learn from experience, debrief, and get better

After you're done with your sales call you need to sit down with your colleagues and go over what worked and what didn't work.

I would take the sequence of events in the process of making a sale — the precanvass, the canvass, the introduction, the need, the need and use, the value, test closing, overcoming excuses, how to wrap the package up, etc. And every time on every step in that sequence I'd hit a bullet point, I'd make some type of analogy with it. "Well, I remember, back in so and so, I did this, and the guy said this, and we did that." Then, another salesman is going to pick up and say, "Well, I took that same idea and, when I went into Home Depot, we did the same thing, but we did this, and it worked out this way." Then I go to point two and do the same. If you've got other ideas or changes, now is the time to add them to the canned talk.

Because you learn sales from experience and only experience. You can't do it in a book. Nobody can teach it to you. So share it with your buddies in the company. Get new ideas from them.

Chapter 5

The Dime Bank Close: Getting to Yes

You know what a close is? It's a thermostat. Tells you if you're getting warmer.

The law of averages is, if you follow the procedure and go through five presentations, you will have an order. That's just written in concrete. But you had to get the multiples going, because you might have to go through 25 to get one or you might get four in a row. But when you add them up, after 100 presentations, if you didn't have 20 orders, you were cheating or not doing the need or not going through the closings.

That's the reason we always shook on partnership. "I'll pay you, providing you do what we train you to do." And if it went through the need with that curriculum guide, and it went through the three closes — four or five if necessary, but a minimum of three closes — guaranteed a hundred bucks every five calls. You just have to get the numbers going for you, get a little proficient, change prospects. So, when we hired someone, we would tell them it takes a hundred calls.

Let's just say, for instance, you have to go to a hundred doors to get in 20, to do 10 presentations. And you go through three closes per presentation, so that meant you went through 30 closes to get an order. Right? Well, that meant, if you had three orders, that would be

300 dollars you made, right? That meant every door you went to was worth three bucks. That meant every door you got in and talked to them or interviewed them was worth 15 bucks. Every demonstration was worth 20 bucks. Every close was worth 50 bucks. So if you kept up those numbers, it's the law of averages guarantees you 300 bucks. Guarantees you a thousand.

Guarantees you five thousand — providing you do the numbers. You had to start with a hundred. You had to start with a bunch. Can't start with five, you know. But that was the law of averages, and it was etched right in stone. And it didn't matter who the person was. I mean, we got old ladies, young kids. But any person that was a family person, I don't care — Protestant, Jewish, religious, black, white, I don't care what the deal was. Even if they were tongue-tied, it was in the numbers — and every product has its numbers.

Getting from the law of averages to an order is a different matter

It's like the proverbial curve in college. Here you are, with a customer who has no interest, right? As I start to show my product, there's going to be a point of optimum interest. At some point, you reach the time to close. Probably only turning up the thermostat on the first attempt to close. But that's the reason you go through three closes — a minimum of three closes. I mean, a test close, a test close, then the close.

The only way you're going to know if you're getting warmer and getting to a sale is to test it. You've got to test it. How are you going to do that? It's with a close. That lets you know, should you stay and you run your gambit, or are you out of gas? Closing is something most salesmen wait to do until the very last minute, hoping his conclusion will get an order. That's the reason they're so disappointed. They're afraid to close up front, because they're scared of a no.

Generally, when they get an "I don't know" they interpret it as a no. "Well, I can't afford that right now." Oh, that's a no; they leave. "Oh, I could never do that without checking with the vice president." Oh, that's a no, and they leave. They're not testing. They're not testing. But if they did, then you would know in what position you'd be in when that optimum time comes.

See, with World Book, we had closes built into our presentation. So, just by turning the pages in my head, I knew I was getting to a close. Before I'd get to a close, I'd have some kind of a trigger to get them up there.

Like I mentioned before, I always place the order pad out front and use it as a notepad and make scratches on it as we talk. And I leave the pen right out. I'm not trying to put it in your hand or any of that. That's cheap selling stuff. You know how some of those people used to get you to sign an order? They drop the pen in your hand, you know. That's a bunch of junk.

With us, the order pad is a negotiating thing. I mean, we're talking and I say, "What's your kid's name?"

"Bobby." I write Bobby's name down. Just fill it out as I go along.

You got to put the order pad out, up front. When I first started, I'd wait and do my presentation, then reach in my bag and go to pull out my order pad. But that spooked them. "Well, what are you doing?"

You want price settled at the beginning

Bringing out an order pad at the end of the close disrupts your sale — another reason you bring it out at the beginning.

The resistance everybody has, even if they want something, is the price. So, let's say you're going in, you're looking at a new Jaguar. You're kicking the tires; you look at the price tag. "Wow! 63,000 bucks?" Now, you know you're going to get it. But you react to the price. And the guy comes up, and says, "May I help you?" What do you say?

The average person says, "No, I'm just looking. I'm just looking."

The average person, even if they want to buy, will be defensive.

But deep down, you are going to buy. You're going to buy a suit, and you see one you like. But then the guy says, "May I help you?" and you say, "No, no, I'm just looking." You don't want to be pressed. You don't want to be pushed.

Believe it or not, the auto industry learned this from us. They used to not have a price tag on the window, but now they do. It's the same as having the order pad out right away.

They used not to do that. Hell, no. But you had to go to the dealer to get the price so you're already preconditioned for the price news. So they've put the order pad out.

Don't be scared of price

Go straight to it. Get it off the table first since that is always the first objection. You do this before he asks how much, because the minute you stop talking, that's the first thing he's going to say when you're presenting something — you're demonstrating something, whatever — I can't afford it. You know it's — price. I mean, you know the price of something, you see something, and you're going to say, "Wait a minute. Whoa! Whoa! How much is it?"

I don't give a darn what the price is, you know what you're going to say. "Hell, I can't afford it. That's too much money."

Okay. So you write the full price down on the order pad, knowing that he will respond with, "I could never afford that." That's where you come in and just smile, agree — heck no, you can't afford that price — which turns the excuse around and you show more material.

Now, how many times should a good salesman close? One more time. That's right. It's always, one more time if you've got a prospect. As long as you all are smiling together, and you're keeping it friendly and light, you can proceed without being pushy. You conspicuously look at your watch, so he doesn't have to look at his, with the comment, "Oh, I have to be brief," "Oh, I'm overstaying my time," "Oh, I'll only take another minute." If you're doing that, he doesn't have to look at his watch.

He's also saying to himself, "Hey, you know, this guy's in a hurry." You actively are trying to diffuse the tension by saying stuff like:

"Hey, I'm going to be brief."

"I'm just going to be a couple more minutes."

And he's saying and thinking, "Oh, man, I can't afford that."

You're anticipating, on the first close, and you're set up for it, and you're begging for the "can't afford it" excuse. You know damned well it's coming. Sure. SATMAC it. Get it off their chest. See, when you get at price, you never get surprised, like, "Oh, I can understand what you mean. Yeah, you've got a beautiful place here, and I noticed that nice car out front — but probably this costs no more than the interest you're paying on your car. But don't worry about it. Let me show you one other thing." Compare it to something; fluff it up. "Buy a cup of coffee today, same as buying the World Books; or like the interest you're paying on your car; no big deal. Like your telephone, you pay for it monthly, we'll let you pay for the World Books monthly. You never lease? Well, hey, you're leasing your phone, aren't you? Don't worry about it. Let me show you one other quick thing. I've got to be brief." You've got to make a comparison, you know.

They have to get it off the chest, up front, so I don't have to deal with it later. So the first excuse is a "can't afford" refusal. Then there is "I've got to see my husband," "Can't afford it, buy it later," "Can you come back?" Whatever they say, you just take it with a grain of salt.

In the beginning, I get that excuse — I can't afford 500 bucks for books! But you don't know that I'm going to sell you a lease for $12 a month. I'm not going to get to that till your excuse gets off, until you say, "I can't afford it." Next, we agree it's too much, and then I shift: "However, if there was a way in which you could work this in, could you see how that would help? In other words, if you could —"

Generally, when people first see price, they're not looking at the savings. But if there was a way to get the savings, where a 10 percent increase in the back room would save you $12 a month, would that equalize the price if we had a way to put it in here for $12 a month?

The dime bank

Okay, understand. That's why we used to carry a dime bank. I always carried three dimes. First, I hand them the dime bank. They'd always take it. "Then I'd say, "What we're talking about is one, two, three . . ." and I drop the dimes into the bank. Easy demo.

"Three dimes a day to put all the knowledge in the Western World at your child's fingertips. He doesn't have to go to the library, doesn't have to stand in line to borrow these volumes kids want most. Don't have to bug your husband. I know he's the smartest man in the world. But the facts are there, just pick up the World Book. Could you put two dimes a day in there and let your husband put one dime in — for all this month? At the end of the month, you'd have twelve dollars, you know."

Dime-bank close. The dime-bank close. Three dimes a day. *Clink! Clink! Clink!* It was built like a World Book, and it looked like a book, and it had World Book on the front of it and a slit in the top — the three-dime bank. You put the dimes in, and they'd go click, click, click. You'd hand it out — and I haven't had a person yet refuse to take it. You got three dimes — I'm going to take them.

And you'd say, "Well, it's as simple as that. All of the knowledge in the Western world, right here at your fingertips — three dimes a day."

"You can't even afford the gas to go to the library for 30 cents, can you?"

The benefits diminish the cost

That's the whole thing. They've got to make a financial judgment, and you've got to diminish that judgment, because she's used to breaking a $20 bill at the store. Mothers used to go to the store with 20 bucks, and they could shop for the week. So we have the right scale, we're saying, hey, what happened to those three dimes, left over? How about the entire knowledge of the Western World for those dimes?

Another one was — I used to love it — I'd say, "Well, you know, it's no big deal. I sure don't want to take food off the table, or anything. But your husband eats lunch out every day, doesn't he? Well, I wonder what he tips the waitress if she's extra nice to him?" and just let that settle in there a minute.

"And that dime bank, three dimes a day, and he's giving her a dollar, and you're sitting with three dimes." It's almost automatic. She says, "Here, I'll get those books!"

Make sure to agree and sympathize

"You said you can't afford a hundred dollars? Well, you know, Doug, that's exactly what I *thought* the first time I saw that. But after Bill showed me this cost savings and how that could offset the cost on this, I started to *think*. And now, with this new *thinking*, I know, for a fact, we can afford it. But let me show you one other quick thing." It's the old set-up — the words and the sequence of those words — *thought, think, thinking.*

"Oh, a hundred — that's a lot of money, but it's probably less than the interest you're paying on that Jaguar." See, I've got them thinking. That's the thing. You want them to start thinking about things for you.

The fundamentals will work — keep pushing

Dime-bank close. There were a million dollars' worth of books sold on three dimes a day. That was our first close. Dime-bank close. *Diminish the cost. Build up the value.* That's what you got to do. You got to diminish that cost. Two bucks an hour, or whatever it was — would that increase productivity by 1½ percent? Now it was free. Now you begin to really start selling, because you have the information to overcome the "can't afford."

Approaching the second close

The reason you didn't drop this on the first close is, it wasn't a real reason. You just play it down. You needed some room and a little time to negotiate and think of how you want to overcome it, so you show them more material. And the second close is to see if the prospect has changed his first excuse and, nine out of ten times, he will. That's what you're checking for on the second close.

So if you play the first one down, "I can't afford them," then you close again, and she's thinking to herself, trying to find another reason, but there isn't one. You know they don't have a reason. They're fishing. They're looking for excuses.

So the first time they say something negative, I've got to see my husband, you slough it off. *The first negative close — all that tells me is, they don't have a reason.* They're looking for excuses.

First one couldn't stop me. Now they're going to change it and come up with something else. Are they stumping me? Nope. Why?

Your buyers are always looking for a reason to say no. But if they're changing their excuse, then they don't have a reason. Now, if they stay with it and stay with it and stay with it, then we'll have to deal with their excuse.

If they're changing their excuse, they're getting weaker. Now, if they hang with it, it might be a reason. And I got to test it. I go back to thought, think, and thinking. How do I get a sentence that uses those words? I need to keep talking and listening — remember, this is why a canned pitch is critical. Flush it out and find out if their excuse is a real roadblock or it's just an excuse that you can break though.

You make some sort of comparison (waitress tips, three dimes, interest payments) when you slough it off. Get it off the table. Then I'd have to work and work and work.

So my second close is to check what's going on. And that's the reason you go through three closes. Is it getting hotter, or is it getting colder? I'm anticipating the "can't afford" or "see husband." Generally, in the business situation, it's a variation of "I've got to consult with" the purchasing agent, vice president. Got to see somebody.

So what do you say here? "You mean you built this multibillion-dollar company out of the trunk of your car? You've got to consult with your accountant to see if you can afford this?" Nine out of ten times, when they give you an excuse, if you give it back exactly how they gave it to you and let it hang there a minute, they'll laugh.

If you get stopped because a prospect says, "My wife needs me," which is a way to say they don't have time to talk to you, well, you say, "Well, I can understand that. Now, let's see what you're telling me. Your wife, who's a mature person, can't get along without you for the next 12 minutes?" Let it hang there.

So, most of the time, if they give you a flippant excuse, if you exaggerate a little bit, throw it back, and let it sit there a minute, they'll probably laugh and say, "Well, not really." And then, they'll come up with something else, you know. So that means they don't have a reason. They're fishing. They're fishing for an excuse to get rid of you.

As long as you're smiling and friendly — but no jokes. *You don't tell any jokes.* Just smile and keep it light.

Now if you stay cool and they get angry, you've got to back off — it's probably time to call it quits. If not, they're getting warmer. They're getting closer to buying.

This is when you move to your second close

You know you're there if you see the prospect change the first stall to another reason. If so, then the first reason was not a valid reason, was it? The next arrow in your quiver is *the lease plan*. You don't discuss that up front. That's your ace in the hole — on a monthly payment plan, or something. Now you compare a minimum payment to something very minute. The profit you get off your worst customer. "Gee, whiz, we're talking about some of the profit you get off of your worst customer. What do you make? Ten bucks a month? That isn't worth screwing with, is it? Well, that's what we're talking about." The interest on your Ford outside; the daily tips you hand out at a restaurant — "That's what we're talking about."

Now, if a person changes the excuse to something different, once again, you SATMAC. You need to feel, in your heart, that you really changed the excuse into a reason to buy. You have to kind of feel that. And the way you do that is with the clinchers. "You'd agree with that, wouldn't you?" "Have you found that to be true?" "Have you seen that — another situation, just like yours?" You know, you get that "Um-hum. Um-hum." Get that going. You want to get the "Uh-huh, Uh-huh," the head bobbing. That's what you're searching for.

Many times, it's good to repeat out loud what they said. Let it hang there but look perplexed, with a big smile, and just kind of let it hang there. "That's what you're telling me? Come on, Frank!" Look surprised. Yeah, you give them the you're-kidding-me look. Let it hang there and smile and laugh, just overcome the stall. *Humor — not jokes.* Very important. As you're smiling and laughing together, you're really not too far apart. He'll feel at ease with you and your pleasant persistence will not be offensive.

Be aware of the body language

I had a whole thing on body language. I think it's very important for salespeople. And they learn it on their own, over a period of time. I mean, you can tell when someone's getting a little uptight — the white knuckles, arms across the chest, fidgeting.

The hardest thing in the world is to just shut up

But shutting up is sometimes the most important thing to do. One of the biggest orders I ever got — a $15,000 deal — was 28 machines.

It was a big deal back then. And I threw the order out there, and he said something — I don't know what it was — flippant. And I overcame it; I don't even know what I said. Then, I said, "Well, Leonard, you know, it's your decision, not mine." And I put the order pad there and put the pen down. And I pushed my chair back, and I had a stare-down. Finally, I knew what he was doing. I said, "You want a cigarette?" And we started laughing together. I said, "Well, are you going to do it or not?" And I shut up again.

And he says, "You son of a bitch." And he signed the order. I mean, it was a big order. I mean, I was 23 years old. Man! The power of shutting up.

When the pressure is on, you have to keep it on. Otherwise, you're going backwards in your pitch

Ask them for the close, and then shut up. It may be a stare-down, or it may not be, you know. But if they're fiddle-fooling around, don't say anything. But don't keep selling. Once you've done your selling, shut up, ask for the order, let them decide if they want to get it or not, or give you an excuse.

Now the best thing to do is listen. Because the minute I throw up any sort of statement, I give him an opportunity to pull out an excuse.

You've been putting them on the spot, and now you're taking them off. Why did you take him off the spot when you put them there? Because no matter what I say, I'm backpedaling and letting him go back to an excuse.

When you get them to the point you've put them on the spot, let them make a decision. But it's the hardest thing in life. I tell people that. "You know, the hardest thing in life is not trying to come up with three dimes a day. Hell, you spend that on Cokes. The hardest thing in life is making a decision, isn't it? That's the reason everybody told me to come and see you. They told me you were a decision maker. And it's a tough decision, but it's your decision. How do you feel about it?" Then shut up. It's his time.

See, now, whoever speaks first loses. If you ask someone a question, like, "Are you ready to order this?" and if they hesitate, and you start talking, well, you've taken them off the spot, haven't you? And you're going to lose the deal, probably. The hardest thing is, when you ask a direct question, "You ready to order this?" or "Can you sign this?" or "Let's go ahead and do this" — when you ask them a question your job is to shut up. And it's common courtesy and respect not to interrupt them and let them think and speak next. And if they wait, it seems like years when it's just a minute. And it's tough. But let them speak first.

Most salespeople let them off because they are afraid of rejection

Don't fear rejection. You know why? Because, worst case, he can dismiss you. You could come back next week, and he'd say, "Look, I didn't want to say no to your face, and I really wanted to get it, but my brother-in-law won't let me." Or "My husband won't let me." So now we're still friends. He's the bad guy, but go away. Let them dismiss you. They'll say something like, "Could you make a call back? Could you come back? Could you come back and see me tomorrow?" That's perfect.

Save your best for last

Offer your doorknob close to bring full pressure, and/or a free trial to grease the skids on this sale.

And the best close in the world — God, it's tough. It is horrible. I've done it on rare occasions, but I've done it. Hold your order pad, you know, we've got Bobby and we've got Jane and we've got the prize and she really wants it, but she's saying, "But I just can't do it. I'm telling you, I just can't do it."

I say — "Well, I know, Ms. So-and-so, you're not saying no to World Book, they're good educational tools and you're really not saying no to Bobby and Jane, your kids, you know. What you're saying no to is the $12 a week, right? Well, I understand, but how do you explain that to Bobby? Better, let me leave this edition with you for a week." That wasn't something I came up with — I learned that from people selling baby pictures — coming around with the pony, take the pictures, then come back and sell you an album. And then, when they start saying no — they'd say, "Oh, I don't know — I can't afford those, but those proofs — could you leave those proofs here?"

The salesman would say, "Well, I'm terribly sorry . . ." Of course, they don't know they've got another set in the car. Man, now, that is tough. I've done it. I don't like doing it, but, depending on the situation, you have to go in for all-or-nothing. No samples, offer the whole set. Make them think about it, the value, then make them think their losing it all, take it away and force them to lose it all. Brutal.

"You weren't saying no to World Book, because you like our books, right? I mean, you love them. And you're certainly not saying no to Bobby — no, certainly not saying no to your kids — it's the $500. What you're saying no to is the $12 a month. And the one that does without is Bobby and Jane, right?" I'm holding the doorknob and that's when they say, "Are you coming back?" and I'm trying to convince them I'm not coming back. The doorknob convinces them I ain't coming back. It's all going away.

Then you go for *the door-knob close*. "How would you like your cake and eat it too?" That means I'm going to give them a free trial. I give them a set to try for three days. What am I doing? I sign them up but I make it a free trial by invoking the three-day cancellation clause.

That's the doorknob close. I'm starting to leave, got my coat on, picking my stuff up. I offer a bonus. Just like you see on TV today. "Here's a hundred dollars' worth of soap. You can have it for 19.95." They're all 19.95. "And if you place the order in the next ten minutes, we're going to double the order." My way? Give them a set for a free, in-home, three-day trial.

That's adding value, on the door-knob, the last chance to get something you probably want anyway but need a little more nudging.

That's the old door-knob close. Double the value, you know, half the price, whatever it may be. We didn't have the privilege of changing price with World Book. One price, one price only — but we could offer that three-day trial.

The puppy-dog close

The free trial saves some sales and it makes others. It gets a salesman in the house of an undecided buyer and it also convinces a husband not to cancel an order. But then there is the puppy-dog close. This one goes like this. "Let me ask you one thing, Ms. Jones. If there was a way in which you could have your cake and eat it too, would you be interested in it? Well, I know what the problem is. The hardest thing in life's making a decision, especially if you don't have support. And you need support if you're going to have some equilibrium with your husband

and in this family, right? Well, I think what you want is this fantastic social and cultural education material for your kids. Your hesitancy is your husband will raise hell. Is that right? He needs to make that decision, doesn't he? Well, we have what we call a 'Mother's Think-It-Over Clause.' We allow you to go ahead and put this on order and you can give him the final decision to cancel. That way, you can show your husband your intentions were good, and your heart's in the right place. Is that fair? And I'll leave you a volume to show him." I probably salvaged more orders that way than anything else.

Again, here, the product is my silent salesman, in my absence. I've got to have something to leave so I leave the A volume. It has animals, aviation, art and architecture. Lots of pictures the kids love. If it's on a Friday, and you need a reason to come back Monday, you leave a copy of the A volume. That way, Monday, come back to pick them up. So you've got a book working for you. You've got a silent salesman working for you rather than them just thinking about the price. They all remember price. But if she has to explain it to the husband or the kids — "Want to see if the kids are going to use it or if they like it," two days in the home, well — didn't do it every time, but it was a hell of a lot better than coming back cold.

IBM did it too. We had 90-day warranty, money back. If you had any dissatisfaction, we'd either get you a new machine or get your money back. But leaving a typewriter there, for three days, for them to use. That's a heck of a lot more better than saying, "I'll just come back with literature." If you have a product that you believe in, then it will do the job. It's your silent salesman.

I call the leave-behind the old puppy-dog close. "Don't buy it. Just take it home and pet it for a while. You don't have to buy this puppy.

Just take it home for a day or two." If you take a puppy in the house for three days, if you've got kids, let me tell you something; that puppy ain't leaving, I'll tell you that. I've got one out at the house right now, peeing all over the place. Chewing up carpet, and everything else.

Big-time companies replicate this tactic. They all do it now. Look at amazon.com or even eBay. Automatic returns, same as leave-behind home trials. Well, when we sold copy machines, it was really crucial because that business was the old Gillette theory: You give them a machine and make your money on service and supplies. Gillette, they used to give you the razor free and make their money on the refills. It's the blade. The old puppy-dog close. We built our company on the trial period. I mean, you're crazy if you don't. If you've got a good product, it'll work.

If you didn't push it hard enough — if you didn't get your influencer excited — you may lose the sale

Buyer's remorse. They just didn't know how to use it right. We took more dictating equipment back to IBM because the secretary didn't like it, and the salesman didn't get in and sell her on the value of it. She preferred to sit on her boss's knee and take it in shorthand, you know. So I lost a few bonuses because they sent it back, after having it in her office for a week. Girl didn't like it. She sabotaged it.

The second sale

But if you do it right, you come back on an installation or a service call and upsell. Once it got in, we always did a service call. With IBM, it was mandatory. When you sold a typewriter, it came in the box, big sign: "Open this box, you lose your warranty." So they'd call us, generally

Friday, at four o'clock. But the idea was we'd go back and unpack them, instruct the operator, solidify the relationship with the operator, and try to sell, you know, on down the road in the same office. That was pretty cool but it was also mandatory.

With World Book, it was not mandatory, but the smart people did it because that's where you got your names and leads and referrals — the service call, the installation — when that big set of books arrived. That's what we call the second sale. And that's the way we used to hire our people. That's where we hired our part-timers. They were so excited about it, and the book had been there for a day or two, by the time we got there, the kids were using them.

We'd bring the kids in and find out their birthday and find out Abraham Lincoln was born then, or Michael Jackson and, you know, look up karate and boxing. There's all kind of stuff in there for kids. So, in five minutes, I could turn a kid on — even one who hated books. I mean, so much fun stuff in there for kids, and it was so well illustrated, I could turn a kid on in five minutes to World Book. Look at the birthdate, karate, boxing, football, Werner von Braun wrote that rocket article. Space was huge. Today it's something else, but whatever it is, it's in there. Every time I went back, I sold an add-on product and made 12 or 15 bucks for my gas, you know. Solidified that feeling with the end user. It works. Definitely worked with copy machines. No question, it worked with copy machines.

This is when you get referrals and upsales. So you'd sell small, to get the order. When you'd come back for the service call. They were so impressed with the product, you'd say, "You think that's something? You ought to see these dictionaries." So we could pick up 8 or 10 or 12 bucks by adding on another product to pay for our service call. The main thing was certainly customer satisfaction, but secondly, was to get names, leads, and referrals. Everybody's got a friend, relative. They'd give us referrals, ten names, or appointments and we'd give them a Bible. I mean, bought them for three dollars or something; they looked like a $50 Bible.

Another way to get the sale — referral deals that let them earn a set

I don't want to take good food off the table. But after a demonstration, they would kill for it, a set of World Books. So we'd say, "Well, if you come to work for us instead of buying and you sell a friend, relative, or neighbor, give up your commission on your third sale, and the company will give you a set." We hired more people like that — I think 90 percent of our full-timers started out coming in part-time to win a set, sold three or four real quick, picked up three or four hundred bucks. Remember, when I started, teachers were making five thousand a year. And so they'd sell three. They'd get commission on the first two, fifty bucks each, or something — and on the third sale they'd get a set. That's the way we hired everybody. It's tremendous.

But only if they're sold on it. Once you do a demonstration, and they would want it, you say, "Here, come on in and earn it. Yeah, we'll give you one." So it was a marvelous, marvelous way of hiring. And, like I say, I personally could have sold them for nothing, because I really believed in the product; really believed in the product.

If you can't make the sale on the spot, it may not be worthwhile to pursue a callback

Callbacks are usually just dead-ends. See, if you decide on making a callback, then they don't have to say no to your face. So first thing you have to do is find out, if you're on a one-on-one situation, if you're going to make the callback or not. And I made up my mind, after about six months in business, I ain't making any callbacks. I made too many and, you know, I have a whole thing on qualifying. I'll make a callback, providing they qualify. If they don't qualify, I ain't making the callback. It's that simple.

Be reasonable about callbacks

Most salesmen aren't. Most of them run out Monday morning. They've got three callbacks. They think they're going to close all three of them. All three of them turned to mush, so they're shot for the rest of the day. So I didn't want people making callbacks first thing in the morning.

Now, the reason they make the callbacks is because they're not getting a no. Every salesman is scared to death of getting a no. To me, the second-best answer I can get, other than a yes, is a no. What I don't want is a callback. The reason is, when a new salesman gets a "can't afford" or "buy later" excuse, they feel it's a no. They don't know how to overcome it. And to avoid a no, they will jump and really wait till it's all over, hoping the presentation will sell itself. Rather than closing on it, they think the books are going to sell themselves — or the typewriter. Rather than hearing a no, they jump at an opportunity to make a callback. Rather than trying to overcome an excuse to push on and keep getting the order, they don't want to be pushy, so people say, "Can you come back?"

Callbacks run more salesmen off than anything else. They get all excited by a callback and think they're going to get this order. They save them till the last day of the month, make 15 callbacks, knowing they're all good, and none of them pan out. So you lose your salesmen.

Even at the corporate level, callbacks are mishandled — nine out of ten times. Here's what they're saying. "I'm not getting a no. Boy, I got a callback, you know." They're hoping, but it's just conversation, hopeful talk, bar talk, something to say to the boss in the sales meeting. "How many are you going to sell this month?"

"Fourteen callbacks. So $800,000 worth." And they're always wrong on their projections.

Callbacks need to be filtered

Only do them if you are actually improving your odds of making the sale. There needs to be new value for you as the salesman. They'll let you come back 14 times. It's your time, your gas, you know. So you've got to have a qualifier. Why come back? When a salesman returns, it's only for one thing. You know it, and they know it. It's for the order. The prospect knows this, but ninety percent of what you said is forgotten, other than the price.

See, if you haven't done your selling on the first call, what are you going to do on the second call, on callback? You going to resell them? You've already sold them. You're going back for a decision. Well, hell, the only thing he remembers when you make the callback is the price. And you got a no the first time. He's forgot everything you told him. What are you going to get on your second callback? "No," is the obvious answer when you make a callback. Even on a sure deal, it turns south on the callback.

Why call back on a non-qualified person? It's your waste of time; it's your waste of gas. Yes, I made tons of them, but only if they qualified. The best qualifier was a wife who was intimidated by her spouse, who would not dare make a decision without her husband.

If I concluded this was real, after many attempts to overcome the excuse, I would say, "Due to my vast territory, how difficult is it going to be for me to get back? I mean, I just can't get back to see everybody twice. Would your husband like to do his job all day long and go back at night and finish it? However, if . . . if I could get back, when would your spouse be home? Nine out of ten times, when would be a time when I could catch him?" Okay. If she could give me the time, then I'd say, "Well, if I did happen to get back, could you arrange it for me to at least come in and sit down and talk to your husband? I won't bug him; I won't hassle him; and I won't put any pressure on him. But if I make the time and effort to come back, would you at least let me come in and talk to him?"

If she comes back with, "Well, he hates salesmen. I don't know. I can't speak for him," and all that, I ain't coming back.

Third one is, "If I do come back, I'm going to show your husband exactly everything I showed you. And if he's a normal human being, I know what he's going to say: 'Well, what do you think, Honey?' Now, when your husband turns and asks you that question, what are you going to tell him?" And I shut up.

Well, if it's "It's his money, he can do what he wants to," I ain't coming back. "Well, I'm going to tell him I want them, and I'll help pay for them." You know, I'll be back in a heartbeat. Be back tonight.

See? No sense in making a callback just because they want to get rid of you. Ask some qualifiers. I would come back under two or three qualifiers. "Well, number one, you've got to guarantee me, if I do come back, that I'm going to get in. I don't want to drive all the way back here at night, you know."

"No, I'll let you in."

"Number two, your husband's got to be here. Will he be here?" And number three, when it's all said and done, "I'm going to show your husband exactly everything I showed you. And I know what he's going to do. He's going to turn to you and say, 'Well, what do you think, Honey?' Now, when your husband asks you that question, what are you going to say?"

For products more expensive than the World Book, a callback was often necessary so that the customer could complete a demo period

I would say 20 or 30 percent of the orders I ever got were on a call-back. Now, I'd say 90 percent in copy machines. Ninety percent with IBM, probably. Because the first round is demonstrations, introductions, and all this stuff — laying the groundwork. So you often have to come back for the order. At that point, you need some support. If he's not willing to give support on the initial call, he sure as hell ain't going to give it on a callback. So be sure he'll say something neutral or positive.

Callbacks can convert to a door-handle close when you use them to generate pressure

After my presentation, the wife, many times, was salivating. She really wanted it. I could tell. And she's using this excuse. So, I would say, "I'd love to come back. Wish I could see everybody twice. But my wife doesn't like me out in the evening. I'm sure, if your husband works eight hours a day, you don't want him to go back to the office every night, do you? Well, my wife's the same way. But let me be quick. I want to show you one other quick thing." She doesn't need to see her husband. I'm talking to the decision maker right now. But I've got to make her believe that I understand that. She doesn't think I do. But I've been married for 20 years. Under it all, I do understand — she is the decision maker.

Depending on the case, sometimes I say, "Well, it's impossible for me to get back. I'm only over in this area once every three months. We have so many calls — our quota — we have to make, and I can't be wasting time on callbacks. So, just tell little Bobby and Jane that I'm terribly sorry. I didn't mean to get him excited about something he's not going to get."

So I've convinced her I'm not coming back. She convinced me she ain't buying. Okay, so it's a stalemate. So I'm leaving. I'm packing up and I always say — "Will you apologize to the kids? I'm terribly sorry. I've done the best I could, and —"

So I put my hand on the doorknob and I say, "By the way, if there was a way you could have your cake and eat it, too, would you be interested? Well, I know you've got to live with your husband, and keeping everything smooth here and all is very, very important. And your husband's going to make the final decision, right? But you've got to kind of set the groundwork, tell him what's best for the kids. We've got a program we call the 'Think-It-Over Clause' for mothers just like you. And we allow you to go in, and we will send you a set, free of charge, up front. You show it to your husband, let the kids try it out, and let him make the final decision. And the final decision is, if he doesn't want it, let him pack them up and send them back. We'll even refund the postage. And that way, you're doing, as a mother, the best you can to get this social and economical beneficial material in your children's hands, and your husband could still be the boss. How's that?"

That's a door-knob close.

I remember one time, I was in Tampa. First started out and saw this wife. Lovely lady, four kids, beautiful situation. She wanted a set of World Books, convinced me she couldn't do it without her husband. It was what we called a late close. We used to take orders into the branch office at 12 o'clock at night.

But, anyway, I'm in Tampa. My branch office is in Orlando. And I'm just starting out learning. And I drove back to where this is, which was 40 miles from where I lived. And I went back to the house, and she came to the door and said, "He isn't home yet. Generally home at 5:00, here it is 6:30, but he hasn't come home yet. But he'll be here in another hour or so, I believe." So I went out and made another call. Went and drank a cup of coffee. Killed some time. Waited till about 8:30. Pulled back to the house. My eyes swept across the front of their house. All of a sudden, all their lights went out.

I've wasted three hours, drove 40 miles. Now I've got to drive 60 miles to Orlando, based on what she told me — twice. That's when I came to the conclusion — I said, "Heck, I'm just not going to torture myself anymore." I was really mad because there were other orders that I had to pick up to take them all in, and it made me run late. If I missed the 12 o'clock deal, they didn't get them on the airplane in time to get them in, and nobody would have gotten their paychecks. So I was mad! So finally, I came to the conclusion — I wasn't in the business six months — I said, "I ain't making any more callbacks."

Don't put your eggs in the callback basket — be tenacious and make a sale right there and now

Well, I'm going to tell you one of the best ones. I'm in this damned house, and the guy's a mechanic. And I never will forget it — down in

Jacksonville. And the mother kind of had me sit in kind of a — back then, everybody took their lean-to garage and made a den out of it. Well, I'm sitting here, and he's in there, and I couldn't get him to come in. TV's on, and he's reading the paper. And every time I'd close on her, feeling she was particularly getting close, I'd hear, "Agh! Hu-agh! Agh!" And she'd ask him if he wanted to come in — "Honey, you want to —"

"No, I don't want to come in. Don't want to come in."

Now, I've got to get this son of a gun in here, or I'm not going to get an order. So, finally, I got him in, and I was, "Hey, Joe, what do you do?"

He said, "Well, I'm the head mechanic down at the Cadillac garage."

And I said, "Well, that's wonderful." I said, "Do you have a manager?"

"Yeah, a young kid." He said, "All he knows he got out of a book. He don't know how to fix anything."

I said, "Well, all he's got is out of a book, but he's still your boss, is that right?"

"Yeah."

I said, "Well, let me ask you something. If your son happened to get really caught on with this school stuff and really started studying and got the — say — he got a scholarship to Michigan State, and he became a head engineer for General Motors. Would you be a little bit prouder of him, or that manager who works for him down at the garage?"

He jumps up and says, "Molly, you'd better get those books." That's a true story.

Make 'em think. Give 'em a thought. Let them start thinking. Keep them thinking about it. *Thought, think, thinking* — the old stuff — and I'm telling you, old stuff still works.

Human nature ain't changed. Technology has, but human nature ain't changed.

Chapter 6

How to Be "A Motivating Son of a Gun"

When it comes to building a sales force, it's not as simple as 1-2-3. Just like clinching the sale, there's no easy way about it. When management looks for a salesman, they're looking for that magic bullet, but he ain't there.

When I would interview people for full-time work, I always looked for someone who had an athletic background. I don't care if it's high school or junior high, whatever. That meant they were *competitive*. If they were competitive, not much is more important than the commission. That's the recognition they learned to love in sports. Then goals? Athletes love busting quotas. A lot of people are competitive and don't even know it. I look for people with a competitive spirit.

So we would interview people and talk about what type of sports and stuff they did in high school or college. Even in the band, it's a competitive type thing. That's what I was searching for — the competitor — are they competitors?

Next is *honesty*. There's "John" and there's "Paul." You'd probably like to deal with John, because he can't exaggerate; he can't lie. His face would crack. Now, it might take two encounters or two appointments before you really get that, but there are certain people that just exude honesty. Most people want to deal with those type people.

Then, you've got old Paul. He'll slap you on the back, "Hey! How you doing, big guy?" and that sort of thing. Well, that works, too. Nothing wrong with that. But I think the sincerity of a person's facial expressions and the way they handle themselves and the way they speak — it's very, very important. More so in commercial selling than it would be in door-to-door.

Women seemed to have these traits in more abundance. My best salespeople at World Book were women. They're smiling, you know, and they just keep on plugging along. And they can put people on a guilt trip. They weren't intimidating. There's a reason women did so well with us. When I started in, it was a pretty tough business. And a gal just didn't intimidate people nearly as much as a man did.

Hiring was "hit or miss." You never know what you have. You might even hire a marijuana farmer. I had a young teacher. He was in college, learning to be a teacher and he was selling some World Books for me, and he came in one day. He said, "Murphy, school's over." And he said, "I've got some plants in my biology class, but Mother won't let me keep them at home. Wonder if I can put them over here, in your office?"

I said, "Sure. Where do you want to put them?"

He said, "I'd want to put them in the back here, in the bathroom, back by the back door."

I said, "Hell, I don't care. Go ahead." So wife comes in one day, to use the bathroom. She said, "Honey, your plants're not getting any sun back here. You'd better put them up front, in the window."

Oh, I'm telling you! So we've got about eight or nine cups, there, in the window. Got a big picture window. So I'm in the Dad's Club, up at St. Patrick's, and there was a guy there, he had the Zenith franchise. We had a poker club, every third Saturday night. And there was a guy that was on the detective bureau at the Police Department. He was in the poker club, he was an undercover detective.

So my turn came up to host. We usually had it at our home but Mama just came home with Cheryl, my daughter. So, I said, "Well, my wife just came back with the baby. Instead of meeting at the house, can we meet at the office?"

Cop said, "Where's your office?

I said, "Up there on such-and-such Avenue."

He said, "Oh, hell." He says, "Got lights on in there?"

And I said, "Yeah."

And he said, "Well, I can't be seen playing poker."

"No big deal." I said, "I've got curtains. We'll pull them."

He said, "Fine." So he comes up, and he looked around. And he said, "What you growing there, Murph?"

And I said, "Oh, it's a teacher of mine. He's doing a project for his biology class, and he wanted to know if he could put them here. And I said sure."

He said, "Oh, I see. Uh-huh." I didn't see him for another week or two in church.

In the meantime, somebody came in and said, "What the hell are you doing with that dope in there?"

I said, "What?" I dumped it all in the commode and told that damned teacher I was about to punch him out. Fired him on the spot. So I saw this cop a couple of weeks later, and I went running up to him. I said, "Man, really, I didn't know that was dope."

He said, "Yeah, I know you didn't." He never did believe me.

Hiring is tough, but that's part of the game. Even the big guys need to churn a lot to find good salesmen. These high types, big guys — Cisco, HP, Proctor & Gamble — they've got the human resources, the assessment tools, the psychologists. And they've got all the profiling in the world. They go find the ultimate candidate. And yet, I would bet their ratios aren't any better than mine. Who I was hiring were genuine people, people that were usually hungry, people who wanted more. Deep down, they were people who wanted the Rolex watch, the Cadillac car, the $400 suit. When you were trying to hire them, you wouldn't take them to McDonald's. You'd take them over here and buy, you know, $14 steak, or something — impress them.

If you hire someone — invest in them

You need to be a mentor and you need to trust them and let them grow. Anytime I ever interviewed anybody for a job, I'd always shake their hand at the end of the interview if I was going to hire them and say, "Let me tell you something. This isn't a job — this is a partnership. And if a partnership's going to last and endure, it's got to be based on what?" And then I'd shut up. What's it based on? *Trust.*

Now, at the end of this guarantee period, I'm going to pay you a thousand dollars — not in confederate or Chinese yen. I'm going to pay you in American dollars, right? Well, your part of the bargain is you're going to guarantee me 20 presentations, 100 calls, do these five closings. But if I catch you cheating, I don't have to pay you, do I? And if you catch me trying to beat you out of the money, you can take me to court, because I'm going to put it in writing. That fair? We've got a partnership. You're not an employee, you're my partner. We'll go out and work together, and I'll show you how to do it. And after you see me do two or three, then I expect you to go off and do them on your own. Is that fair? I'm not equal, but I'm going to try to be fair."

I'd hired them but I'm trying to make my point. "I expect you to do so many calls, so many closes, and it's a partnership, it's built on trust. I'm not going to be with you every day. I have to assume you're going to do it. But if I catch you cheating and turning in fake orders or fronting orders or any of this crap, I'm just going to negate this guarantee. That fair? If you do it, I guarantee I'll pay you."

Trust is better than a time card

A partnership has got to be built on trust. If it ain't, it ain't going to last. Been that way for years — everybody I hired, you're not my employee, you're my partner.

There's nothing like an inspiring mentor

I had a mentor once too. There was a guy that was his own manager at the time, and my branch manager with World Book in Florida brought him down to talk to me. And I met him. And I'll give you background on him in a minute. Very humorous Italian guy.

After I met him, the very next year, Marshall Field sent him to Australia and gave him a five-year project: Hire so many people, sell so many books, work out these supply chains, get warehouses, do — the whole continent of Australia. Whatever his job was, he accomplished it in three years. They brought him back to Chicago. He was in Chicago six months. He was man of the year in Chicago. Dynamic son of a gun.

When he came back, Marshall Field set him up in field cosmetics — they were going after Avon — because he was so dynamic, and women loved him. For some reason or other, that company didn't fly. I don't know.

He was with them for a year or two. So he came back and ended up being president of the company. And if anybody that motivated me, it was him. He was a motivating son of a gun.

You and your employees need to believe in the product

This includes believing you aren't "taking food off the table" at anyone's house. I believed in World Book. I was raised on it, as a kid. It's a communicator, greatest communicator in the world. Werner von Braun would talk in a way that the average high school graduate could never understand. World Book was the bridge to bring that knowledge into an understandable language. Each article in World Book is written at a grade level. If you're studying the pioneers and patriots in the third grade, it's for the third-grade level. If you're studying Sequoia or some in-depth African tribe, or something for junior high, it would be at the seventh-grade level. If you're into physics or chemistry or biology, it would be at the high school level. So each article was graded, based on its relevance to school. And it just made a lot of sense, and all three of my kids were raised on it.

Yeah, so you're not taking food off the table. Our price was very, very fair. Britannica Encyclopedia was a thousand. We were 500. And what are you talking about, 12 bucks a month? Heck, who is that going to break? I could push on it, because they really didn't have to make a sacrifice to get World Book. When I started, it was eight bucks a month. When I left, I think it was 25 a month, something like that. So, as inflation went on, and people started making better money, World Book was never a deal of buying it and not paying for your food or paying your bills. It never was. Never was. And I knew that.

Motivating employees means you need to pay them

They need to understand the value of commissions, how that payment structure isn't different from getting paid twice a month on salary I hired them under a minimum draw. And I think, back then, it was maybe 200 a week. World Book had a plan that was called Management Development — MDP program. And they were paying people $200 a week salary plus commission plus bonus plus overrides. And that's how we hired principals or teachers or coaches away from their job, under a guarantee.

A guarantee is a tightrope

You need to pay people enough to keep them from suffering but not enough that it extinguishes their hunger for more. They have to be comfortable, not looking over their shoulders. Pay the rent. But they have to have five sales a month, part-time. And once they knew they were there, we'd bring them in — try to bring them in full-time.

It's all the law of averages. Now, I questioned it too, at first. I didn't think it would work for me. It worked for everybody else, sure, but not for me. That's what you think going in. But after so many presentations, I said, "Well, that works for me because I'm doing it; wouldn't work for anybody else, but it works for me." What a change.

Now I train them. And the biggest compliment I get usually comes a year later. I catch my guy training a new person and he's telling *my* jokes. You know, they're telling *my* stories. It's a great compliment. That's how it goes, though. Once you get some sales under your belt, well, now you know you can do it, you're part of a special fraternity, and it starts to be fun. Like I said, selling isn't hard, you work the averages.

Keeping a new salesman

Okay, you promised them all these wonderful things. He's going to get a Jaguar, and he'll have a big house, and all that stuff. So, how many calls did you make with him?

That's the secret. You keep salespeople by going out and letting them see you fail. See, that's what they want to see. They tell me, "Well, let's go to this house. I was just kicked out of there. Let's see what you can do."

"Like heck," I say. "I don't want to get kicked out. Let's go next door."

But that's what they want to see, see? What they're saying is, "Oh, you're sitting in that big office. You're the hot shot, but you didn't get thrown out, you don't *really* know how embarrassing it is."

"Well, heck! Let me go with you." That's what they love. They want to take you to a place where they throw me out, physically.

Go in the field with them. That's the way you keep them.

That's what I love to do. People said when I was a manager, "Oh, you're living off my work. You just want me to work harder so you can make more money."

I said, "Look. We've got a sales contest coming up next week. Here's ten bucks. Guaran-gauran-damn-tee I'll outsell you." And every time I went to Boston, Tampa, Jacksonville — wherever I went, I made, right in the first of the month, a big spiff about going out and outselling their top salesmen. Then I didn't have to sell any more. I didn't have to prove myself any more. And that, to me, is another secret of keeping salespeople.

So you train them. And then, after a while, you'll see them training someone, and they're telling your jokes or your experiences or your stories. You laugh.

Have a plan

Once you've got your sales force ready, you need to have a plan. That plan must be tailored to your product. I took my daughter to the fairgrounds and saw a Ferris wheel, and nobody was on it. It would go for a minute, and it would stop; go for a minute and stop. Next day, we came back, and the Ferris wheel was spinning, and there were a thousand people in line. What was the difference? The difference was the people yelling and screaming. They were drawing people, they attracted attention. The first guy you put on, run that thing till someone else comes up and stop, put them on, run you up till someone else came up. Pack it and then it's automatic.

The concept I got out of that was you start working in January, like 12 cars on a Ferris wheel, to fill up February and March. Then you start working in February to fill up March, April, and May. By the time you get around to August, you've got more places to call on than you can shake a stick at.

Motion begets motion, action begets action. But people don't do that. "What can I get today? I want an order today. I want an order this week." Try working for the future. Try a plan. And after three or four or five months, you'll see — have places to go. Working for the future.

Working for the future starts with an honest appraisal of what your sales cycle is going to be

If you're selling Avon or a Lincoln Library for $39, you want that sale right now. You don't want to get in and talk and demonstrate. You ain't got time. It's a question of numbers.

But if you're selling a $500 product, like I was, you got to get in and talk and sit down and negotiate. And if you're selling a $10,000 computer, you're not going to waltz in and get an order in two minutes. That's going to take three or four calls. So it depends on what you're selling. Then plan around that.

Selling copy machines would be selling the future, lining up things. World Book, can't do that. You've got to get the order right there. That's the reason you can be immediately successful, selling a $500 product. Where, if you sell a $10,000 or $12,000 — $80,000 product, like real estate, it takes you a long time to build that client base and get referrals and — takes you a long time to make it go.

There're *three types of sales*. One is the incremental, dime-bank-type thing, where you can do it now. Then there's a long-term, calling on Toyota, calling on CSX Railroad, where your selling big, $10,000, $20,000, $100,000 equipment, you're not going to waltz in and do a presentation and walk away with an order. It ain't going to work that way. So there are three types of selling.

Inexpensive stuff

The little $29 Bible — you don't want to get in and talk to demonstrate. It's "Wham-bam, thank you, Ma'am," type thing, like you're selling Avon. You do it on the doorstep. Because you have such an appealing product at a cheap price. The commission's low so you need to sell a lot and fast. Again, it's a question of numbers. Just like an infomercial. You just throw enough out there. You know it's going to hit certain places. Move along when it doesn't work. No time.

Mid-market stuff

But when you're selling a little bit more pricey product, you've got to take a little bit more time, use a little bit more energy, be a little bit more professional. That's the $500 and $800 and $900 product.

Very expensive stuff

When you're selling a $20,000 or $30,000 product, you ain't going to waltz in and walk out with an order — unless you have laid some very serious groundwork. A quick sale will only happen when there is already great potential.

Expensive things will have a long cycle

That's fine. Plan for it and use it to your advantage. I mean, on copy machines, the guy that bought one a year and a half ago, and it's on a three-year lease, he doesn't need another one today. But, I'm telling you, I know, in another 14 or 15 months, he's going to be upgrading. So I'd keep a log. So that's part of working a territory.

There's no such thing as a wasted call

You and your organization need to remember that eliminating prospects is almost as important as identifying them. In either scenario, you are getting closer to a sale. Get rid of a non-prospect, focus on a definite good prospect, a possible future prospect.

That's the difference between a salesman and a professional salesman. You need to understand the value in all the information your organization brings back, even if it doesn't lead to a hot prospect. You need to break down these calls — someone who needs to buy now, someone who needs to buy soon, and someone who needs to buy in a while. Sort of break them out in thirds.

Track your results across the board

Your team won't get better unless you do. Keeping score — people never do it. Let me ask you something. You bowl?

What's your score? Play golf? What's your score? You made 35 calls last week. What's your closing ratio?

Almost no one can answer that question. Nobody keeps score. You wouldn't dare bowl without keeping score, and you wouldn't play golf without keeping score. But you'll make a hundred calls and say, "Let's see. I think I got two sales. And I don't know what it was. I got a one out of five, or a one out of nine — I don't know. I don't keep score." Why not? The most important activity in life is making a living. Why don't you keep score? Are you ahead of the curve or behind the curve?

If you don't make a living, you lose your house, your wife, your family, your kids. I mean, what's more important? The most important thing in life is making a living. It's a war out there. And nobody keeps score in sales.

But professionals do. You've got to know what your average is. How many calls, cold calls, how many were not home? If you can do five demos a day, you'll get an order a day. And, man, I had some of the biggest dummies, and most of them were teachers. It would be like a light going on. "Wow! You told me one out of five. I did 15 presentations and got three orders. But I went ten and didn't get any. But my last five, I got three."

"You got one out of five, didn't you?"

Yep! It's like a light turning on. And once they are sold on the law of averages, then I'd convince them: "Every demonstration you do puts 20 bucks in your pocket. Every door you knock on, you made a buck and a half. So you'd better knock on more doors, right? Better do more presentations."

We would constantly underscore the value of a door, the value of a demo, the value of your law of averages.

Forget sales. If you do the numbers, they'll come. They always come.

Epilogue

Jim Murphy lives in Shelbyville, Ky. with the family he loved for so many years. The joy that he found selling spilled over to the next generation of Murphy's including son Jim who trained under his father than started his own company, now a successful corporate training and consulting firm in Atlanta, Georgia.

Door-to-door selling remains one of the most difficult and certainly one of the most awkward sales experiences anyone can have but it reflects at lot of larger truths about selling anything to anybody in any business. Whether you are in outside sales at a restaurant chain, inside sales at an airline or a hotel chain, or selling sophisticated data mining software for some multi-billion dollar tech company, it all begins and ends with people. Satisfy what they need. Deliver what they want. Let them know how your product solves their problems or it makes them look smarter. Jim Murphy used simple real-world examples and a low stress sales approach to hit customers right in the heart of their wants and desires. It worked then, it works today, and it will work again tomorrow.

So, Ladies and gentlemen, start selling.

Made in the USA
Middletown, DE
11 July 2015